The Peaceful Classroom

162 Easy Activities to Teach Preschoolers Compassion and Cooperation

By Charles A. Smith, Ph.D.

Illustrations by Nancy L. Downing

gryphon house
Mt. Rainier, Maryland

© 1993 Charles Smith

Cover Design: Beverly Hightshoe
Cover Illustration: Cheryl Kirk Noll

Published by Gryphon House, Inc.
3706 Otis Street,
Mt. Rainier, Maryland 20712.

Library of Congress Cataloging-in-Publication Data

Smith, Charles A.
    The peaceful classroom : 162 easy ways to teach preschoolers compassion and cooperation / by Charles A. Smith : illustrations by Nancy L. Downing.
        p.   cm.
    Includes bibliographical references and index.
    1. Group work in education. 2. Education, Preschool—Activity programs. 3. Education, Preschool—Parent participation.
I. Title.
LB1140.35.G74S64 1993   93-22372
371.3'95—dc20   CIP

Contents

Preface 10
Introduction 12
    About the Peaceful Classroom 13
    How Activities Are Structured 14
    Letter to Parents 15
    Suggestions for Success 16
    Friendship Skills, Definitions and Examples 17
    Compassion Skills, Definitions and Examples 17
    Cooperation Skills, Definitions and Examples 18
    Kindness Skills, Definitions and Examples 18
    Friendship Activities Organized by Skill and Age 20
    Compassion Activities Organized by Skill and Age 20
    Cooperation Activities Organized by Skill and Age 21
    Kindness Activities Organized by Skill and Age 22
Recommended Reading 24

Chapter One: Belonging and Friendship

Letter to Parents 26
3+ Name Chanting 27
3+ Roll Over 28
3+ Child in the Dell 29
3+ Name Fame 30
3+ Classmobile 31
3+ Magnet 32
3+ Classy Tree 33
3+ Our Group 34
4+ Name Game 35
4+ Musical Names 36
4+ Frankenclass 37
4+ No Word 38
4+ School Garden 39
4+ Sound Waves 40
4+ Our Feet Treat 41
4+ Still Water 42
4+ My Friend 43
4+ Knock, Knock 44
4+ Hand Pictures 45
4+ The Magic Pocket 46
4+ My Family 47
4+ Missing Person 48
4+ Class Flag 49

4+ Penelope's Present 50
4+ Whose Shoes? 52
4+ Come Over 53
4+ Guess What Happened! . . 54
4+ Name Pantomime 55
4+ Our Rising Stars 56
4+ Family Show and Tell . . . 57
5+ The Class Gallery 58
5+ Mystery Person 59
5+ Mystery Voices 60
5+ Whose Hands? 61
5+ What You Wear 62
5+ My Mobile 63
5+ Getting to Know You 64

Chapter Two: Compassion

Letter to Parents 66
3+ Emotion Pictures File . . . 67
3+ How Do **You** Feel? 68
3+ Make a Face 69
3+ The Little Lonely Star . . . 70
3+ Poor Little Sad Eyes 71
3+ Sad Teddy 72
4+ Happy/Sad Person 74
4+ Emotion Tags 75
4+ Emotion Drawing 76

4+ We Half Feelings 77
4+ Emotion Puppets 78
4+ Happy/Sad Sticks 79
4+ Contrasting Feelings 80
4+ Face Plates 81
4+ I'm Happy Sometimes . . . 82
4+ I'm Sad Sometimes 83
4+ I'm Afraid Sometimes . . . 84
4+ I'm Angry Sometimes . . . 85
4+ Emotion Dancing 86
5+ Feeling Face Masks 87
5+ The Sound of Feelings . . . 88
5+ Emotion Stories 89
5+ Whose Feeling 90
5+ Emotion Picture Studio . . 91
5+ Really Feelings 92

Chapter Three: Cooperation

Letter to Parents 96
3+ Mouse on the Run 97
3+ Dough It Together 98
3+ Double the Fun
    (or How to Find a Partner) 99
3+ Juicy Group 100
3+ Butter Lover 101
3+ We're All Winners 102
3+ Class Nature Collage . . . 103
3+ Hand Me Pictures 104
3+ Group Soup 105
3+ Tug of Peace 106
4+ Rockabye 107
4+ Cookie Machine 108
4+ Balloon Bounce 109
4+ Puzzles for Us 110
4+ Balloon Pick-Up 111
4+ Back Stand 112
4+ Basket Catch-It 113
4+ Body Drawing 114
4+ Stick Together 115
4+ Two Islands 116
4+ Bubbles in a Basket 117
4+ Cat and Bird 118
4+ Cooperative Towers 119
4+ Chair Jam 120
4+ Telephone Friends 121
4+ Crossing the Bridge 122
4+ Hot Potato Stories 123
4+ Rope Runners 124
4+ Cooperative Drawing . . . 125
4+ Pick Up With Sticks 126

4+ Carry Board Teams 127
4+ Over the River 128
4+ Roller Ball 129
4+ Class Garden 130
4+ Not Enough 131
4+ Won or Two 132
4+ Jet Plane 133
5+ Rocket Ship 134
5+ Rubber Band 135
5+ Mule Team 136
5+ Copy Cat 137
5+ Card Partners 138
5+ Partner Kickball 139
5+ Drop in the Bucket 140
5+ Peace Table 141

Chapter Four: Kindness

Letter to Parents 144
3+ Growing Flowers 145
3+ Plant Life 146
3+ Adopt a Tree 147
3+ Gentle People 148
3+ I Cannot See 149
3+ Nature Tribute 150
3+ Bird Dinner 151
3+ Growing Up 152
3+ The Ouchie 153
3+ Know See 154
4+ Lotion Motion 155
4+ Are You Sick? 156
4+ Hospital Gifts 157
4+ Food for the Hungry . . . 158
4+ Rescue Chain 159
4+ Kindness Coupons 161
4+ Blind Kind 162
4+ Wishing Well 163
4+ Give a Lift 164
4+ Flower Power 165
4+ Birds in the Trees 166
4+ Generous for Us 167
4+ Wonder Wands 168
4+ No Stranger to Danger . . . 169
4+ Staying Safe 170
4+ Ship in the Night 171
4+ Know Talk 172
4+ Seeing I's 173
4+ The Goonfalla Trap 174
4+ The Touch Toe Path 176
4+ Get Well 177
4+ Sheet Carry 178

4+ Sad Person 179
4+ The Star Seat 180
4+ Look, No Hands 181
4+ Know Hear 182
4+ Gentle Breeze 183
4+ I'm Mobile 184
5+ Giving Free 185
5+ Night Train 186
5+ Sprain Pain 187
5+ Dream Catcher 188
5+ Yay Say 190
5+ Taste Helpers 191
5+ Touch Me 192
5+ Cats and Mice 193
5+ Roly-Poly and
        the Kind Fairies 194
5+ No Walk 196
5+ Night Flying 197
5+ Parachute Rescue 199
5+ Mama Hen 200
5+ Forest Tag 201
5+ Farmer Brown
        and the Rabbits 202
5+ Left Out 204
5+ Princess (or Prince) Gentle 205

Index 207

Preface

My first book, a textbook titled *Promoting the Social Development of Young Children*, was published in 1982. In addition to the typical academic fare found in any textbook, the book included 111 activities to promote body and sensory awareness, emotional development, affiliation, conflict resolution and kindness in young children. These activities, with their emphasis on how children's beliefs about themselves and others influence relationships, were based on my experience teaching young children at Purdue University, Bowling Green State University and Texas Tech University

Promoting the Social Development of Young Children went out of print in 1988. In 1991 I received a call from the Peace Corps who was interested in the book. The Peace Corps had recently established a program in Romania to assist care-takers working with abandoned or orphaned children living in large institutions. The new government was concerned about the emotional, social and moral development of these children who were growing up in difficult circumstances. Some Peace Corps volunteers felt my book would be of value in their work.

This call inspired me to revise and republish the material found in the original text. Instead of simply repackaging material, I wanted to make four significant improvements to strengthen the new book. First, I would emphasize positive social behavior. Activities for the textbook that focused exclusively on body and sensory awareness would not be included. The best activities on social development from the textbook would be retained. Numerous additional activities would be created to expand on this core. Second, practicing teachers would be the primary audience for the new book. Instead of theory and research, the new book would emphasize large and small group activities that could easily be implemented by teachers of young children. Third, the format of the activities would be expanded to include picture books that complement the activities. Stories of friendship, compassion, cooperation and kindness are powerful tools for reaching a young child's mind and heart. Fourth, every activity in the book would offer suggestions for involving parents in the educational program.

Parent involvement is an important element in *The Peaceful Classroom*. Each of the 162 activities in this book include at least one suggestion for reaching out to parents. Each section begins with a letter to parents you can reprint or re-write to introduce parents to what you hope to accomplish. I am looking forward to hearing about the innovative ways you reach out to parents including newsletters, bulletin boards or sending notes home with children.

I would also like to hear the stories you have about these activities and how children responded to your efforts to nurture friendship, compassion, cooperation and kindness. I too have stories to tell: about the two young boys in my class who were my "seeing eye dogs" while I wore a blindfold; about the shy young girl who took me for a walk outside on another occasion when I was blindfolded; about the young boy with cerebral palsy who crawled across the floor during circle time to reach and hug a classmate whose affection had just been rejected by another. Write to me in care of the publisher if you are interested in sharing your experiences in *The Peaceful Classroom*.

Although I have assumed much different responsibilities since the original textbook was written, my heart will always be in the classroom, on the floor with young children, telling stories, offering puppet shows, talking, hugging, laughing. To these and all the other children who taught me about kindness, I extend a sincere thank you. I would also like to thank those teachers who participated in my university courses and workshops and whose enthusiasm and dedication inspired my efforts. I especially appreciate the support and insights provided by my friends Lois Bates, a daycare teacher and Andrea Scheib, a home day care provider. Thanks also to Carolyn Foat, Bill Carver, Sue Morrow, Anne Ahlenius and Kitty Beverly, all exceptional teachers who touched my life over the years.

I would also like to express my appreciation to the professionals at Gryphon House, especially Larry Rood and Kathy Charner, for their guidance and enthusiasm. Finally, I owe a debt of kindness to my family: Betsy, Sarah and Bill for the chorus of support I needed to complete this project.

Introduction

Teachers of young children are at the beginning of the wonderful life-long enterprise of nurturing a human spirit. What we do has the potential to endure over time, long after a child has left our care.

Do you remember the first time a child called you a "teacher"? How did you react? Were you surprised? Were you proud? "Teacher!" a child declared, and the whole world changed for us. At this moment we became someone who had power and magic in the eyes of a young child. With such power came the responsibility to provide the best for children entrusted in our care. We became a companion and advocate for children in their learning journey. We became real teachers, not just baby sitters or drill instructors. Real teachers do more than fill children's heads with numbers, shapes and letters of the alphabet. These skills are important. But real teachers change lives. To change lives, we have to reach out to childen's hearts as well as their minds. We have to create a place of safety where children are free to investigate the world around them, to discover their inner landscape of emotions and to explore human relationships. By emphasizing non-violence, compassion and the understanding of our shared humanity, we create *The Peaceful Classroom*.

We can use spontaneous opportunities to help children understand themselves and others. A bird feeding its young, two armies of ants locked in combat, a child with a skinned knee are opportunities to learn about life and the human condition. We can also encourage children to explore the give-and-take nature of human contact during free play. As they experience this social laboratory, children learn about the consequences of compassion and cruelty, cooperation and competition.

We can also create and introduce planned experiences at classroom centers and in small groups. In these more structured situations, we can teach children the skills that will enable them to live peacefully and productively with others. Group experiences provide a safe context for children to observe, try out new skills and practice what they have learned.

By weaving planned activities with more spontaneous encounters, we can create a powerful and responsive learning environment that encourages friendship, compassion, cooperation and kindness in young children.

About *The Peaceful Classroom*

The Peaceful Classroom provides 162 classroom activities for children from about three to five years of age, although they can be used with children up to age eight. Activities are organized into four chapters: Friendship, Compassion, Cooperation and Kindness. Each chapter explores three or more skills:
Friendship: Association, Conversation, Belonging, Friendship
Compassion: Recognition of Emotions, Problem Solving, Expression
Cooperation: Cooperation, Consideration of Others, Negotiation
Kindness: Caretaking, Gentleness, Helping, Generosity, Rescue/Protection, Respect/Encouragement

Each of the four themes build upon each other, providing a foundation for those that follow. In general, Friendship activities provide a foundation for Compassion, Cooperation and Kindness.

Within each chapter, activities focusing on one skill prepare children for those that follow. For example, association activities should generally precede those focusing on belonging.

In addition, activities within each chapter are listed in the order of age complexity, beginning with those appropriate for three year olds and older and concluding with those for five year olds and older.

There are many ways to use this book. One way is to do all the activities in the book developmentally appropriate for your children. Start with the first activity in the Friendship chapter, then continue in sequence until the activities become too difficult. Then move to the first activity in the second chapter, Compassion, and continue as before until the activities become too difficult. Repeat with the chapter on Cooperation and finish with Kindness. This strategy provides the greatest scope over the longest period of time.

Another approach is to choose one chapter. Begin with the first activity and stop when they become too difficult for your children.

Choosing activities for a specific skill like gentleness or association is another way to use the book. There is a list of activities for each of the sixteen skills beginning on page twenty. Activities for any single skill are often found in more than one chapter.

Designing your own strategy is always a good way to proceed. If you have a specific issue in mind and a limited amount of time, you can choose and introduce activities in a developmentally appropriate sequence. If you teach three year olds, for example, and want to focus on "appreciation and respect for the environment," you could do the following activities:
Growing Flowers
Plant Life
Adopt a Tree
Nature Tribute
Bird Dinner
Classy Tree
Class Nature Collage

You can assemble activities around such issues as sensitivity for disabled people and celebration of racial and ethnic diversity. The basic skills of friendship, compassion, cooperation and kindness can be combined in various ways to address nearly any social issue of concern to you and your parents.

How Activities Are Structured

Skills developed
One or more specific skills targeted by the activity.

Introduction
Background information regarding the skills and suggestions for implementing the activity.

Age
The minimum age for the activity. This is only a baseline. Older children should begin with the simpler activities, gradually leading up to the maximum for their age.

People words to use
Terms likely to be used and learned during an activity.

Center
The location suggested for the activity: Circle time, Art, Science, Kitchen, Movement (open space in the classroom), Outside. Where more than one is listed, the children move from one to another in the order listed.

Things you will need
A list of materials you will need to accomplish the activity successfully. In every case, the materials are readily available or simple to prepare.

What to do
A step-by-step explanation of how to introduce and complete the activity. Suggestions as to what a teacher might say and do are provided. Consider this section as an illustration of the intent and approach of the experience. How you actually implement the activity should reflect your own unique style as a teacher.

Want to do more?
Whenever possible, this section comments on the activity's limitations or strengths and suggests ways to make it more successful. Many activities can be made simpler for younger children or more challenging for older ones.

This section may also include a recommended children's book related to the activity's general theme. In addition to reading the book in your classroom, you can recommend it to parents for reading at home.

Involving parents
The best educational programs create a partnership between teachers and parents. In addition to the letter on page fifteen, a "Letter to Parents" is provided at the beginning of each chapter. Feel free to rewrite these letters to make them more suitable to your specific group of parents. Use these letters to introduce parents to your emphasis on friendship, compassion, cooperation or kindness. Every activity also includes a brief suggestion for involving parents in the education of their children. You can give these suggestions to parents when they pick their children up at the end of the school day, or prepare a sheet of instructions for them.

Dear Parents,

We are looking forward to having your children in our class this year. They are ready and willing to learn. We want to provide a quality educational program that inspires them to create, discover and achieve.

Keep in mind, though, that the best educational programs do more than just teach children how to count and say the alphabet. These programs reach children's hearts as well as their minds. Self-esteem and effective relationships are important goals for our program.

We want to work with you this year to make a real difference in your children's lives. We want each child to feel a part of our school group, to make friends and play cooperatively with others. We will help them learn about such basic human emotions as happiness, sadness, anger and fear. We will encourage them to respond compassionately to others during emotionally difficult moments. We also hope that they learn to treat others with respect and gentleness, to be generous and to offer help when possible. This is our "peaceful classroom."

You and your child are important to us. Success depends on establishing an effective partnership between home and school. We will keep you informed of our progress and will suggest activities you can do at home to provide continuity with what we are doing at school. We are eager to hear of your concerns as well. Let us know what is important to you.

We care deeply about being teachers. We feel honored to be a part of your children's lives. We are also aware of the great responsibility we have as partners in teaching and nurturing your children.

Sincerely,

Suggestions for Success

Personal comfort
Activities should make sense to you as the teacher. You should be comfortable with what you select. If you feel uncomfortable about introducing an activity, choose another.

Group and individual match
Activities should meet the needs and interests of the group and individual children. At the beginning of the year, "name" games are useful since children may want to get to know each other better. Some activities may be too threatening or confusing to children early in the year when they are still strangers.

In concert
Different types of activities can be used "in concert" with each other to increase their impact. To emphasize cooperation, read a story about two children working together, organize cooperative painting, and lead the children in a cooperative fingerplay. Look for different ways to bring the activities you do in your classroom "in concert" with each other.

Sequencing
The activities in this book are listed in their approximate order of complexity. Keep in mind that children may respond better to some activities if they have been properly prepared by one or more previous activities. "Blind Kind," for example, should be preceded by "I Cannot See" and "Know See," both of which prepare children to wear blindfolds.

Readiness
Children should never be physically or psychologically pressured to participate. They are likely to become willingly involved if they know what to do, and you are prepared and enthusiastic. Sometimes a group may be ready, but individual children may be unwilling to participate. If so, be prepared to direct them to another supervised activity away from the main group.

Flexibility
Your effectiveness as a leader depends on your ability to adjust as the activity unfolds. Children may react unpredictably, or an unexpected learning opportunity might occur. Be ready to adjust your activity plan spontaneously to overcome problems or to take advantage of favorable circumstances.

Safety
The well-being of children should be your highest priority in everything you do. Every safety precaution should be taken as you invite children to participate in classroom activities. Eliminate hazards like sharp objects if you involve children in large muscle play. Supervise the use of scissors during art play. Be vigilant whenever blindfolds are used. Remain alert to these and other potential problems and observant of every child in your group.

Friendship Skills, Definitions and Examples

Association
Recognizes others who belong to the school group.
Example:
- "Sally and Zoe go to my school."

Conversation
Attracts and holds the attention of others in socially acceptable ways; Engages in positive conversations with peers.
Examples:
- A child taps another child on the shoulder and asks her a question when she turns around.
- "Hello, Jamie. Would you give me the crayons?"
- "Sally, c'mon—you can play 'trucks' with us."

Belonging
Identifies relationships within their primary family group; Understands why families are important; Expands their sense of belonging to include groups other than their immediate families; Forms a group identity that embraces everyone in the group; Uses the terms *us* and *our* to refer to the entire group; Will lead and follow others in the group; Recognizes when someone is absent from the group.
Examples:
- "My daddy's name is Chuck, my mommy's name is Betsy and my sister's name is Sarah. We are a family." "Families are important 'cause the mommies and daddies feed their babies."
- "Pioneer School is my school, and this is my class, and Mrs. Penner is my teacher."
- "Everyone here is in Mrs. Wilson's class. She is our teacher."

- "Teacher, where is Cindy? She's not here today."

Friendship
Get to know and be known by other individuals in more personal ways.
Examples:
- "Mark really likes chocolate cake. I like white cake."

Compassion Skills, Definitions and Examples

Recognition of Emotions
Uses visual and auditory cues to recognize happiness, fear, sadness and anger.
Example:
- A three year old points to another child who is crying and says to his mother, "He sad."

Problem Solving
Describes happiness, sadness, fear and anger; Identifies circumstances that affect emotions, the consequences of emotional behavior and effective ways to express one's own emotions and respond to the emotions of others.
Examples:
- A five year old describes sadness as feeling like "...there are tears in your heart."
- A four year old says, "When I feel sad, sometimes I cry."
- A seven year old comments, "When you get mad, it doesn't do any good to hit—they might hit you back."

Expression
Finds words to describe his or her own emotional experiences; Responds emotionally to loss, danger, frustration and gain; Responds to his or her own emotions with effective, compassionate action.

Examples:
- While watching a television show, a three year old runs to her mother and says, "I scared, mommy."
- When he finds his pet canary dead in its cage, a four year old cries.
- When he starts to get scared watching television, a five year old leaves to play in his room.

Cooperation Skills, Definitions and Examples

Cooperation
Understands the word "cooperation"; Works together with others to solve a problem or reach a common goal; Understands that actions are interrelated and are mutually beneficial.
Examples:
- "Look, teacher, Terry and I are cooperating!"
- Three children work together to clean up the block area.

Consideration of Others
Makes adjustments in behavior to accommodate another person; Shows awareness of another person's goals.
Examples:
- Child moves over at a crowded table to make room for another.
- Child runs slower to let a partner catch up.

Negotiation
Makes suggestions for preventing or resolving a conflict; Describes consequences of another's behavior; Describes circumstances surrounding a conflict.
Examples:
- "We all want the balloon. So let's take turns."
- "Michael, if you play so rough somebody might get hurt."

- "They are fighting because Nancy took his truck."

Kindness Skills, Definitions and Examples

Caretaking
Understands the basic needs of plants, animals and people; Learns simple steps for nurturing the growth of plants, animals and people; Understands *well*, *sick*, *hurt* and *taking care of*; Describes steps for restoring health following illness or accident; Learns simple skills for easing distress and restoring health.
Examples:
- "Flowers need water to grow."
- A child feeds her pet hamster every day.
- "Teacher, my tummy hurts and I feel sick."
- "When you are sick, your mommy takes care of you."
- "When you are sick, you stay in bed and eat soup until you are better."
- A child prepares a tray of crackers and orange juice for her sick mother.

Gentleness
Understands the harmful consequences of careless or aggressive behavior toward the environment, plants, animals and people; Treats the environment, plants, animals and people with respect and tenderness.
Examples:
- A child carefully holds a guinea pig in his arms, avoiding sudden or squeezing movements.
- A preschooler gently puts his arm around a crying classmate to comfort her after she falls down.

Helping

Can identify how to help someone solve a problem; Assists another to achieve his or her goal; Expresses appreciation to others.

Examples:

- "If Jamie cannot reach the shelf, I could get it for him because I am taller."
- "Here, teacher, I can help you pick up the crayons you dropped."
- "Thanks for your help, Sandy."

Generosity

Differentiates between *mine, yours* and *ours*. Derives satisfaction from ownership; Feels secure about their belongings;

Makes sacrifices by giving what they own to someone in need;

Examples:

- "Don't take that truck. It's mine. I brought it from home."
- A child takes her friend to her room and says, "See, Sandy, all these toys on this shelf are mine. Everything over there belongs to my sister."
- A child gives his friend one of his cookies and says, "Here Mark. You don't have any cookies so I will give you this one."

Rescue/Protection

Can differentiate between safe and dangerous activities; Removes threats to the safety of another person; Can think of effective strategies to prevent harm to the environment, plants, animals and people; Intervenes, when possible, to prevent harm to the environment, plants, animals and people.

Examples:

- "Matches are dangerous. They can burn you."
- A child removes a pin he sees on the floor so that his baby brother will not hurt himself.

- "You stay safe by playing in the front yard and not going out in the street. A car could hit you in the street."
- While playing on swings in the park, a kindergartner tells two first graders to stop teasing her younger brother.

Respect/Encouragement

To esteem the environment, plants, animals and people; Motivates others to reach a goal; Shows pleasure with the accomplishments of others.

Examples:

- "Teacher, isn't the tree beautiful?"
- "C'mon Preston, you can do it!"
- "Wow, Marcia. You sure are a good runner!"

**Friendship Activities
Organized by Skill and Age**

Association

Three year olds
Name Chanting 27
Roll Over 28
Child in the Dell 29
Name Fame 30
Classmobile 31
Magnet 32

Four year olds
Name Game 35
Musical Names 36
Still Water 42
My Friend 43
Knock, Knock 44
Whose Shoes 52
Come Over 53
Name Pantomime 55
Get Well 177

Five year olds
Mystery Voices 60
Whose Hands? 61

Conversation

Four year olds
No Word 38
Hand Pictures 45
The Magic Pocket 46
Guess What Happened! 54
Get Well 177

Five year olds
Copy Cat 137
Card Partners 138
Peace Table 141

Belonging

Three year olds
Classmobile 31
Classy Tree 33
Our Group 34

Four year olds
Frankenclass 37
School Garden 39
Sound Waves 40
Our Feet Treat 41
My Family 47

Missing Person 48
Class Flag 49
Penelope's Present 50
Our Rising Stars 56

Five year olds
The Class Gallery 58

Friendship

Four year olds
My Family 47
Family Show and Tell 57
Telephone Friends 121

Five year olds
Mystery Person 59
What You Wear 62
My Mobile 63
Getting To Know You 64

**Compassion Activities
Organized By Skill And Age**

Recognition of Emotions

Three year olds
Emotions Picture File 67
How Do **You** Feel? 68
Make a Face 69

Four year olds
Happy/Sad Person 74
Emotion Tags 75
We Half Feelings 77
Contrasting Feelings 80
Face Plates 81
Sad Person 179

Five year olds
Feeling Face Masks 87
The Sound of Feelings 88
Emotion Picture Studio 91

Problem Solving

Three year olds
The Little Lonely Star 70
Sad Teddy 72

Four year olds
Happy/Sad Sticks 79
I'm Happy Sometimes 82
I'm Sad Sometimes 83
I'm Afraid Sometimes 84

I'm Angry Sometimes 85
Sad Person 179

Five year olds
Emotion Stories 89
Whose Feeling 90
Really Feelings 92

Expression

Three year olds
How Do **You** Feel? 68
Make a Face 69
Poor Little Sad Eyes 71

Four year olds
Emotion Tags 75
Emotion Drawing 76
Emotion Puppets 78
I'm Happy Sometimes 82
I'm Sad Sometimes 83
I'm Afraid Sometimes 84
I'm Angry Sometimes 85
Emotion Dancing 86

Five year olds
Emotion Picture Studio 91

Cooperation Activities Organized by Skill and Age

Cooperation

Three year olds
Roll Over 28
Classy Tree 33
Mouse on the Run 97
Dough it Together 98
Double the Fun 99
Juicy Group 100
Butter Lover 101
We're All Winners 102
Class Nature Collage 103
Hand Me Pictures 104
Group Soup 105
Tug of Peace 106
Adopt a Tree 147

Four year olds
Frankenclass 37
School Garden 39
Sound Waves 40
Class Flag 49

Penelope's Present 50
Emotion Drawing 76
Emotion Dancing 86
Rockabye 107
Cookie Machine 108
Balloon Bounce 109
Puzzles for Us 110
Balloon Pick Up 111
Back Stand 112
Basket Catch-It 113
Body Drawing 114
Stick Together 115
Two Islands 116
Bubbles in a Basket 117
Cat and Bird 118
Cooperative Towers 119
Chair Jam 120
Telephone Friends 121
Crossing the Bridge 121
Hot Potato Stories 123
Rope Runners 124
Cooperative Drawing 125
Pick Up With Sticks 126
Carry Board Teams 127
Over the River 128
Roller Ball 129
Class Garden 130
Jet Plane 133
Rescue Chain 159
Ship in the Night 171
Sheet Carry 178
Gentle Breeze 183

Five year olds
Rocket ship 134
Rubber Band 135
Mule Team 136
Copy Cat 137
Card Partners 138
Partner Kick Ball 139
Drop in the Bucket 140
Night Train 186
Parachute Rescue 199

Consideration of Others

Three year olds
I Cannot See 149
Growing Up 152
Know See 154

Four year olds
Rope Runners 124
Cooperative Drawing 125
Carry Board Teams 127
Over the River 128
Blind Kind 162
Wishing Well 163
Birds in the Trees 166
Know Talk 172
Seeing I's 173
Look, No Hands 181
Know Hear 182

Five year olds
Copy Cat 137
Card Partners 138
Partner Kick Ball 139
Sprain Pain 187
Roly-Poly and
the Kind Fairies 194
No Walk 196
Night Flying 197
Left Out 204

Negotiation

Four year olds
Two Islands 116
Cooperative Towers 119
Crossing the Bridge 122
Rope Runners 124
Carry Board Teams 127
Over the River 128
Not Enough 131
Won or Two 132

Five year olds
Partner Kick Ball 139
Peace Table 141
Left Out 204

Kindness Activities Organized by Skill and Age

Caretaking

Three year olds
Growing Flowers 145
Plant Life 146
Adopt a Tree 147
Nature Tribute 150
Bird Dinner 151
Growing Up 152
The Ouchie 153

Four year olds
Are You Sick? 156
Give a Lift 164
Gentle Breeze 183

Five year olds
Sprain Pain 187

Gentleness

Three year olds
Magnet 32
Class Garden 130
Growing Flowers 145
Plant Life 146
Gentle People 148
Nature Tribute 150
Growing Up 152

Four year olds
Still Water 42
Stick Together 115
Jet Plane 133
Lotion Motion 155
Are You Sick? 156
Give a Lift 164
Wonder Wands 168
The Touch Toe Path 176
Sheet Carry 178
Gentle Breeze 183

Five year olds
Sprain Pain 187
Taste Helpers 191
Touch Me 192
Cats and Mice 193
Roly-Poly and the Kind Fairies 194
Forest Tag 201
Princess (or Prince) Gentle . . . 205

Helping

Three year olds

The Little Lonely Star 70
I Cannot See 149
Know See 154

Four year olds

Body Drawing 114
Crossing the Bridge 122
Kindness Coupons 161
Blind Kind 162
Know Talk 172
Seeing I's 173
The Toe Touch Path 176
Look, No Hands 181
Know Hear 182
I'm Mobile 184

Five year olds

Taste Helpers 191
Roly-Poly 194
No Walk 196
Night Flying 197
Mama Hen 200

Generosity

Three year olds

Nature Tribute 150

Four year olds

Won or Two 132
Kindness Coupons 161
Hospital Gifts 157
Wishing Well 163
Flower Power 165
Generous For Us 167
Get Well 177
Sad Person 179

Five year olds

Giving Free 185
Dream Catcher 188
Left Out 204

Respect/Encouragement

Three year olds

Poor Little Sad Eyes 71
Nature Tribute 150

Four year olds

Wonder Wands 168
Get Well 177
The Star Seat 180

Five year olds

Yay Say 190
Forest Tag 201

Rescue/Protection

Four year olds

Rescue Chain 159
Birds in the Trees 166
No Stranger to Danger 169
Staying Safe 170
Ship in the Night 171
The Goonfalla Trap 174
Sheet Carry 178

Five year olds

Night Train 186
Roly-Poly 194
Night Flying 197
Parachute Rescue 199
Mama Hen 200
Forest Tag 201
Farmer Brown and
the Rabbits 202
Princess (or Prince) Gentle . . 205

Recommended Reading

Chase, L. *The Other Side of the Report Card: A How-to-do-it Program for Affective Education.* Pacific Palisades, CA: Goodyear, 1975.

Fluegelman, A. *The New Games Book.* Garden City: Doubleday, 1976.

Fry-Miller, K. and Myers-Walls, J. *Young Peacemaker's Project Book.* Elgin, IL: Bretheren Press, 1988.

Hunt, M. *The Compassionate Beast: What Science is Discovering about the Humane Side of Humankind.* New York: William Morrow, 1990.

Johnson, D.W. and Johnson, R.T. *Learning Together and Alone: Cooperation, Competition, and Individualization.* Englewood Cliffs: Prentice-Hall, 1975.

Kohn, A. *The Brighter Side of Human Nature: Altruism and Empathy in Everyday Life.* New York: Basic Books, 1990.

Orlick, T. *The Cooperative Sports and Games Book.* New York: Pantheon Books, 1978.

Orlick, T. *Winning Through Cooperation.* Washington, DC: Acropolis Books, 1978.

Prutzman, P., Burger, M.L., Bodenhamer, G., and Stern, L. *The Friendly Classroom for a Small Planet.* Wayne, NJ: Avery Publishing Group, 1978.

Rubin, Z. *Children's Friendships.* Cambridge: Harvard University Press, 1980.

Schulman, M. *The Passionate Mind: Bringing Up an Intelligent and Creative Child.* New York: The Free Press, 1991.

Smith, Charles A. *From Wonder to Wisdom: Using Stories to Help Children Grow.* New York: New American Library/Penguin, 1989.

Wuthnow, R. *Acts of Compassion: Caring for Others and Helping Ourselves.* Princeton: Princeton University Press, 1991.

Chapter One

Belonging and Friendship

Dear Parents,

As we begin The Peaceful Classroom program this year, our first emphasis will be on belonging and friendship. We would like to help your children learn the following:

The names of other children in the class;
How to attract and hold the attention of others in a pleasant way;
That they are an important part of our school group;
How to invite each other to play and make friends;
How families are different and why they are important.

We will use words like "names," "class," "group" and "belonging." Children will participate in activities like "Name Chanting," "Classmobile," "Magnet" and "Frankenclass." We will also be reading carefully selected picture books that focus on belonging and friendship.

Children with high self-esteem are comfortable with their sense of belonging. They feel nurtured and accepted by others. They reach out self-confidently because they believe they can contribute. Skills in this area provide a foundation we can build on as the year progresses. Our emphasis now on belonging and friendship will complement all other areas of our educational program.

Can you remember some of the friends you had as a young child? What kinds of play did you most enjoy? Did you make friends easily or did you find it difficult? Do you remember what it felt like to be left out? Learning how to get along with others is not an easy task. We have all had to learn how to cope with rejection, how to give and take, and how to bring others into our lives.

There are many ways we can work together to nurture your children's talents for making friends. One of the most important things you can do is to share memories with your child. Also, many of the activities we do at school can be tried at home. We will keep you informed of our progress and would like to hear any suggestions you might have.

Sincerely,

Name Chanting

3+

All children love to hear their name spoken by others. As they listen and clap in unison to the beat of each other's names, they begin to develop a sense of community. Do not use phrases that might embarrass a child. Begin the activity with your own name.

What to do

1. Make up a brief rhyme for each child's name (nonsense rhymes are fine). For example:

   Anne, Anne, bought a pan.
   Peter, Peter, pumpkin eater.
   Sarah, Sarah, fe fo farah.
   Bill, Bill, climbed a hill.

2. Slowly chant each rhyme twice and clap your hands to the beat of each word, for example: Peter, Peter, (two claps) pumpkin eater (two claps).

3. Look directly at the child whose name is being chanted. The speed of the chant and clapping can be varied.

Want to do more?

You can ask older children to think of words that rhyme with their names, for example, Mike/bike. Another child or the teacher then makes up a chant for the group to repeat. For example, "Mike, Mike, rides a bike." Or dispense with the rhyme altogether. Ask a child to name something she likes to eat and make up a rhythmic chant incorporating her preference, for example, "Sarah, Sarah, loves ice cream."
• Read *George and Martha One Fine Day* by James Marshall (Houghton Mifflin, 1982).

Involving parents

Suggest to parents that they try this activity at home with their children. Name rhyming might be especially fun while riding in a car.

People words to use

name
together
community

Center

Circle time

Things you will need

• Nothing

Roll Over

People words to use

names
group
class
gentle
together

Center

Circle time

Things you will need

- One medium-sized rubber ball or foam ball

Gathering in a circle is a great way to build a sense of group identity among children. Adding a song or chant increases the feeling of togetherness. Even a simple activity like rolling a ball back and forth calls for the give-and-take necessary for pleasant association with others.

What to do

1. Form a circle with the children standing and ask them to hold each other's hands gently. Ask them to chant with you:

    Hands together,
    Hands together, make a group, (Join hands)
    Hands together, make a group,
    All together, here we stand, (Hands now joined)
    This is our group, so lend a hand. (Raise joined hands)

2. Make a tight circle and sit. Take out the ball and tell the children you will slowly roll it to someone across from you. When that person catches the ball, everyone in the group should say her name in unison. That person then rolls the ball to someone else. Continue until everyone has been named. Repeats are acceptable as long as everyone is named at least once.

Want to do more?

Create and practice a melody for the chant. • With older children, the child who catches the ball can name the child who rolled it. • Introduce last names or name an item of clothing worn by one or more of the children. A child then rolls the ball to the child so identified. • The "Hands Together" chant can be used any time you form a circle. • Read *Whispering in the Park* by Fred Burstein, illustrated by Helen Gogancherry (Bradbury Press, 1992).

Involving parents

Encourage parents to talk about their childhood friends with their children. What did their friends look like? What did they enjoy doing with them? Parents can draw a picture of a childhood friend and ask their children to do the same. Tape both pictures up on the refrigerator.

Child in the Dell

3+

This activity is patterned after the traditional "Farmer in the Dell" game, substituting children's names for farmer, wife, nurse and so on. If you have more than ten to twelve children, you might consider stopping after about half the children have been selected. The activity can be repeated later that day or the next to include those not named. You may also divide the children into two groups if another adult is available.

What to do

1. The group forms a standing circle, and one child is selected to begin. This child goes to the center of the circle, and others sing while they move in a circle around her. For example:

   Sarah in the dell,
   Sarah in the dell.
   Hi ho the dairy-o,
   Sarah in the dell.

2. The song continues in its familiar manner with the named child pointing to another. For example:

   Sarah picks Michael,
   Sarah picks Michael.
   Hi ho the dairy-o,
   Sarah picks Michael.

3. As in the original song, the last child is asked to stand alone while the others return to the group.

   Tom stands alone,
   Tom stands alone.
   Hi ho the dairy-o,
   Tom stands alone.

Want to do more?

Try reversing the rules by starting with everyone clustered together in the center of what will become a circle. The first child skips around the group while the rest of the children chant. From the outside of the group, the first child points to another child. When the chant is completed, they join hands. Gradually a circle will form around the remaining children. The final verse ("stands alone") is not chanted.

• Read *My Friend John* by Charlotte Zolotow, illustrated by Ben Shecter (Harper and Row, 1968).

Involving parents

Prepare a short descriptive list of the children in your group, naming each child and giving addresses and phone numbers (with permission). With four year olds and older, briefly interview each child: What do you like to eat? What is your favorite toy? What do you like to watch on television? Include the replies for each child. Parents can go over this class list with their children at home.

People words to use

names
group
class
circle
alone

Center

Circle time

Things you will need

• Nothing

Name Fame

People words to use

names
group
class

Center

Circle time

Things you will need

• Nothing

Naming activities are easier when the entire group participates simultaneously. Once children are more familiar with each other's names, they are more likely to be confident enough to respond alone.

What to do

1. Ask the children to stand, holding hands in a circle. Move around inside the circle while the entire group chants:

   Think real well,
   We hope we don't miss.
   Think real well,
   Now who is THIS?

2. Just before the word "THIS," stop and stand directly in front of one child. After the chant is finished, the group shouts the child's name in unison. This procedure can be repeated until everyone is named.

3. Once they are familiar with the rules of the game, children can take turns making the selections.

Want to do more?

Make the activity more difficult by choosing a child to go around the circle from child to child during the chant. On "THIS," the moving child stops and has to name the child she is facing. • Read *Jenny's Bear* by Michael Ratnett, illustrated by June Goulding (Putnam, 1992).

Involving parents

Encourage parents to invite their children to make a picture to send to one of their friends on the class list. Use the class list to address the envelope.

Classmobile

3+

Some parents may be unable to obtain pictures of their children. If you think there might be a problem, borrow a Polaroid camera to take pictures at school. Polaroid pictures establish some consistency in quality and ensure that all children are included.

What to do

1. Before class starts, obtain photos of similar size for each child in your group. Punch a hole in the center top of each picture. Tie one end of a single piece of yarn through this hole. Suspend the coat hanger from the ceiling near where the group will meet.

2. Call the children together and invite them to help you make a "classmobile" to hang in the classroom for all to see. The mobile will consist of photos of everyone who belongs to the group. Ask one child to name everyone in the group.

3. Take out the pictures and ask the group to name each person whose photo you hold up. Tie the pictures to the hanger at different heights. When finished, encourage children to comment on the activity. Hang the mobile at a height and location where they can see it.

Want to do more?

The children can draw self-portraits on large index cards. Hole punch the cards and hang them with yarn as you did the photos.

Involving parents

Parents can make a similar "Family Mobile" at home, using photos or self-portraits.

People words to use

class
group
belonging
pictures
names

Center

Circle time

Things you will need

- One photograph of each child and teacher in the group
- One hole punch
- Various lengths of yarn, one for each picture
- One coat hanger

Magnet

People words to use

names
group
class
gentle touch

Center

Circle time

Things you will need

- Nothing

Ask children to be gentle when they touch the "magnet." Try the variation with children who dislike the physical attention this activity involves.

What to do

1. Ask the children to join hands in a circle. When the music begins, the group skips or walks around while continuing to hold hands. When the music stops, call out a child's name. Everyone immediately breaks hands and runs to surround and gently touch the named child (the magnet).

2. As soon as the last child makes contact, begin the music again. Everyone joins hands in a circle and repeats the activity.

3. Continue until all the children have been named.

Want to do more?

Instead of touching the child, the rest of the children can join hands around her, chanting:

Hello _____, hello _____.
How are you? How are you?
Hello _____, hello _____.
We like you too!

Immediately after the chant, begin the music again and repeat the activity. • Read *That Bothered Kate* by Sally Noll (Greenwillow, 1991).

Involving parents

Parents can help their child "write" a note to mail to one of their classmates. Older children can invent their own spelling, and younger children can dictate what they want to say. The children can also decorate the envelope and mail the letter.

Classy Tree

3+

This activity provides an excellent opportunity to emphasize the importance of treating nature with respect. Point out to children that the branch was no longer useful to the tree. Taking a branch from a live tree would not be the right thing to do.

What to do

1. Find a suitably large branch on the ground in a wooded area. (Take the children with you, if possible.) Strip all the dead leaves from the branch and insert the base into a bucket of sand for support.

2. Gather the children around the "tree" for circle time and ask them if they think something is missing. Suggest they make some pretend leaves for the tree from pictures of their hands. Invite the children to go to the art area where construction paper and other materials are available.

3. Trace around the children's hands, using as many colors of construction paper as possible. Ask them to cut their "hands" out and write their names on one side. Tape a piece of string to the middle finger of each paper hand.

4. Assemble the children with their cutouts in a circle around the tree. Ask the children to hold up their leaves. As they do so, say something like, "Just like leaves that belong to one tree, each of you is a special person in this class." Ask each child to stand, one at a time, and select a place on the branch to tie their cutout hand. Help, if necessary.

5. Find a safe place for the tree, where it is clearly visible but well out of harm's way.

Want to do more?

Instead of finding a real branch, paint a tree on a large piece of butcher paper and tape it to a wall or bulletin board. Each child can put one hand in finger paint—spread on a sheet of finger painting paper—and make an impression on one branch of the tree. • Consider using other materials to represent the children: photos, ribbons, footprints, etc. • Read *Jackie's Lunch Box* by Anna Grossnickle Hines (Greenwillow, 1991).

Involving parents

Show parents your class creation and suggest they make a similar "Family Tree" at home.

People words to use

group
individual
person
class
belong

Center

Outside
Circle time
Art area

Things you will need

- Several colors of construction paper
- Scissors
- Crayons
- Length of string for each child
- Tape (or stapler)
- Large branch
- Bucket and sand

3+

Our Group

People words to use

group
individual
class
belong

Center

Art area
Circle time

Things you will need

For each child:

- One empty checkbook box
- Two or three small rocks that will fit inside the box
- One 6" paper plate
- Tape
- Crayons
- Glue
- Scissors
- Construction paper and other decorative materials

The presence of a set of dolls representing children in the class reassures every child that he or she is an important part of the group.

What to do

1. Set materials out at the art table. Ask each child to draw a picture of his face on his paper plate. Place the rocks inside each box and tape securely shut. The rocks should weight the bottom of the box when it is set on end. Glue the center of the paper plate to the top front of the box. The children can then decorate their "figure" with clothes made of construction paper and other decorative materials.

2. When all the figures are completed, ask the children to bring them to circle time, held near a suitably long shelf. Invite the children, one at a time, to place their figures on the shelf. When all the figures have been placed, say something like, "Here is our class, our group. Here is each one of us. Every day, when we first meet at the beginning of class, we will use these figures to help us remember who is in our group. You may take your figure back to the art area to make different clothes, but do not take anyone else's figure."

3. Each morning, you can ask the children to take and hold their figures when they first meet as a group. The remaining figures will remind the children of who is absent.

Want to do more?

Other types of figures can be made. For example, a styrofoam ball can be decorated and glued to a tall plastic bottle. • Older children can shade the paper plate to approximate their skin color. • Read *Voyage Under the Stars* by Bernadette Gervais and Francisco Pittau (Lothrop, 1992).

Involving parents

Parents and children can make a similar set of "dolls" at home and display the doll family in a special location.

Name Game

4+

Rhythmic chanting and clapping can be used to help children learn each other's names early in the school year. Maintain a relatively fast tempo throughout this activity.

What to do

1. Begin with the naming chant and ask the group to repeat it with you. In this example, a teacher named Ann selects Sue to begin.

   Ann, Ann, look at everyone—
   Point to Sue, and then you're done.

2. After pointing to Sue, the teacher asks Sue to find Bill.

   Sue, Sue, look at everyone—
   Point to Bill, and then you're done.

3. Now Bill becomes the pointer. The activity continues until all children have been named. The last child can be asked to point at the teacher to complete the activity.

Want to do more?

For added interest, make simple construction paper flowers for each child. Instead of simply pointing, the selected child can approach and give the named child a flower.
• Children's names can also be placed in a container passed around the circle. Each child would draw and announce a name for the chant. The teacher would begin, and from then on, the last child named would become the "pointer."

Involving parents

Children can dictate to their parents a brief letter to one of their friends in the class. They can also decorate both the letter and the envelope before mailing them.

People words to use

names
class
group
chant

Center

Circle time

Things you will need

• Nothing

Musical Names

People words to use

names
group
class
partner

Center

Movement area

Things you will need

- Music
- A chair for each child minus one

In this variation of musical chairs, everyone remains in the game. Regular musical chairs can distress children who are forced to leave the game and watch from the sidelines. All children like to hear others mention their name. Play the game several times to give everyone an opportunity.

What to do

1. Arrange the chairs in a circle. When the music stops, the child who cannot find a chair stands behind someone seated in the circle. Once everyone is positioned, the standing child names his seated partner.

2. In each successive round, remove a chair. After the halfway point, two or more children will be standing behind each seated child. Each of the standing children should say the seated child's name, one after the other.

3. At the end of the game, one seated child will be named by the rest of the group.

Want to do more?

For variety, reverse the movement of chairs: start with one, then add one each turn.

Involving parents

Encourage parents to arrange with the parents of one of their child's classmates for the children to visit after school or on a weekend. Parents should involve the children in planning activities for the visit.

4⁺

Frankenclass

Make several different "Frankenclasses" if there are more than ten children in your group. Arrange them side-by-side.

What to do

1. During circle time, tell the children you would like to give them the opportunity to work together to make a very special "paper person." Tell them that this person will be composed of drawings of everyone in the class. The children decide which part of the body they would like to be. One child can be the left hand, another the right foot, another the head and so on.

2. Have each child lie on the butcher paper so you can draw an outline of the chosen body part. Ask the children to cut out their names and put them on their parts of the body for the "Frankenclass." The children can decorate each part with paint or crayons. The parts of the body should then be taped or stapled together to hang up on the wall.

3. Use the occasion to discuss the range of physical differences among children in the class.

Want to do more?

Glue the parts of the body onto styrofoam and then glue the pieces together to make "Frankenstatues."
• Read *Best Friends* by Miriam Cohen, illustrated by Lillian Hoban (Macmillan, 1989).

Involving parents

Send home a length of butcher paper so parents and children can make their own "Frankenfamilies."

People words to use

group
individual
class
belong

Center

Circle time
Art area

Things you will need

- Crayons
- Paint
- Butcher paper
- Tape or stapler
- Scissors

No Word

People words to use

communicate
talk
ideas
sounds
sign language
deaf

Center

Circle time

Things you will need

• Nothing

Young children are very egocentric and often have difficulty understanding the implications of a disability they cannot see. This activity will help them appreciate the importance of the senses in communication.

What to do

1. Prepare sign language that you can teach your children to represent simple words:

   I (point to yourself),
   like (hug yourself),
   help (cup hands together)

   eat (bring hand to mouth),
   see (cup hand over eyes),
   you (point to child)

   this (point to object),
   daddy (stroke imaginary beard),
   mommy (stroke imaginary long hair)

2. Talk with the children for a few moments about deafness. "You know, some people cannot hear. When the birds sing, they cannot hear their music; when lightning flashes in the sky, they cannot hear the thunder...." Continue with your own examples.

3. Take a moment just to listen quietly to nearby sounds. Emphasize that a deaf person cannot hear these sounds. "But even though they cannot hear what you say, many deaf people learn what's called sign language, a way to talk using your hands. I have made up some words for my hands. Watch what I do with my hands and tell me what I'm trying to say to you."

4. Choose a very simple statement to act out, for example, "I see you." (Point to yourself, then to your eyes, then to a child.)

5. Ask the children to tell you what they think you are trying to communicate. Go over each word one at a time. Invite the children to repeat your actions as you do them.

6. Add a few more words to your shared vocabulary. Combine the actions in three-word sentences and ask them to guess their meaning.

7. Invite the children to make up their own sentences.

8. After you have about nine words in your vocabulary, ask the children to create actions to represent additional words.

Want to do more?

Increase the complexity of this activity by expanding the vocabulary and increasing the number of actions in a statement. • Emphasize that what the children are learning is not the language deaf people use to sign. Invite a deaf person who knows how to sign to your class to talk with the children.

Involving parents

Describe the activity to parents and keep them informed of the words you are learning. Encourage them to use sign language in conversations at home. Parents may be able to suggest other actions to represent words that children can teach the group at school.

School Garden

4⁺

A garden is a good metaphor for a group. Each flower is separate and beautiful yet contributes to the loveliness of the whole. Although young children are not likely to understand the connection between metaphor and reality, working together to make a common product, and visibly demonstrating their togetherness makes this type of activity important.

What to do

1. Using different colors of construction paper, cut out a variety of stems, leaves and simple flower shapes.

2. Spread the butcher paper across the tabletop and set out the plant parts. With the children's assistance, draw the "ground" for the class garden across the length of the paper.

3. Starting at one end of the sheet, assemble your flowering plant from the cutouts by pasting them to the "ground" on the butcher paper. Write your name inside your flower. The children then take turns assembling and adding their flowers to the class garden. Each child's name should appear somewhere on his flower.

4. After all the flowers are assembled, invite the children to draw a sun, clouds, birds, bugs and butterflies in the garden.

5. Once completed, the garden can be taped to a wall or tacked to a wide bulletin board.

6. Within the next few days, conduct a circle time near the garden. Emphasize that just as each flower in a garden is special, so each child in the class is special. Point out the uniqueness of each flower.

Want to do more?

The children can cut out the stems, leaves and flowers themselves if they are old enough to manipulate the scissors. • Add decorative detail to the flowers by drawing on them with crayons.

Involving parents

Send home construction paper for parents to make "Family Gardens" with their children.

People words to use

group
together
individual
class
belong
unique

Center

Art area
Circle time

Things you will need

- A large sheet of butcher paper
- Several colors of construction paper
- Scissors
- Crayons
- Glue or paste

Sound Waves

People words to use

group
individual
class
belong
taking turns

Center

Circle time

Things you will need

- Nothing

Be prepared for some real silliness here. Laugh along with children. If they have a difficult time going around the circle, explain the idea of taking turns.

What to do

1. Gather the children into a circle. Tell them that you would like to see if they can make some "copy cat" sounds, something we may call "sound waves." To illustrate, step forward into the circle and make a simple sound with your voice. Ask everyone to say it together. Then go around the circle, each child making the sound, one after another until everyone has had a turn. Then ask for someone to volunteer to make a different sound for everyone to copy.

2. The sequence is repeated with each volunteer: the child makes a sound, everyone says the sound together, and the sound wave goes around the circle.

Want to do more?

To make sound waves easier, ask the children to pass a ball as they make the sound. As soon as they get the ball, they should repeat the sound and pass the ball to the next person. • With older children, start two different sound waves in opposite directions around the circle. • Or instead of a sound, try a "body wave," moving one part of the body: arms, hands, legs, feet.

Involving parents

This would be a fun activity for parents and children to play in the car, excluding the driver, of course.

Our Feet Treat

4⁺

The logistics of this activity are a little complicated. Make sure to change the water frequently. Do not pressure any child who does not wish to participate.

What to do

1. Stretch the butcher paper out on the floor in the art area. Tape it down at the ends and at several points along the edges. Place a different color of paint in each pan. Set the chair at one end of the paper.

2. Call the children to the art area. Show them the paint and butcher paper. Tell them you are going to help them make a "Feet Treat" to hang in the classroom. You will be the first one to show them what to do.

3. Take off your shoes and socks and sit in the chair at the head of the paper. Ask a volunteer to take a paintbrush. Choose a color and ask the volunteer to paint the bottom of your feet. When both your feet have been painted, turn to the paper and carefully stand on it with your feet fairly close together. Sit back down and wash, rinse and dry your feet.

4. Slide the chair down slightly and ask one of the children to start. That child chooses another child to paint her feet. Help each child stand up to avoid slipping and falling.

5. The completed painting should be a row of everyone's feet. After drying, label the feet and hang the "Feet Treat" along one wall in the classroom.

Want to do more?

Allow the children to walk around on the paper instead of making a row of feet.

Involving parents

Parents can use fabric paint to make family-feet shirts.

People words to use

group
individual
class
belong

Center

Art area

Things you will need

- Two plastic buckets of warm water, one soapy
- Several towels
- Three or four colors of tempera paint
- Three or four pans
- Wide paintbrushes, one for each color
- Small chair
- One long sheet of white butcher paper
- Tape

MS. BROWN   ANDRE   JANET   TIMMY   AMY

Still Water

People words to use

names
gentle
group
class
blindfold
volunteer

Center

Circle time

Things you will need

• Blindfold

This activity works best with small groups. With a group of more than nine, do the activity until about half the children have been blindfolded. The others can have a turn the next day.

What to do

1. Form a small circle of five to nine children. Explain the rules for the activity. Blindfold a volunteer who stands in the center of the circle. The rest of the children hold hands and begin walking in a circle while softly chanting,

   "Around, around, around we go, and where we stop _____ (name of blindfolded child) won't know!"

2. After a few moments, the child in the center of the circle says, "Still water!" The circle then stops moving. The blindfolded child walks forward until she touches someone in the circle. After exploring the other child's head and clothes, the blindfolded child tries to guess that child's name.

3. That child may choose to go into the center of the circle to begin the game again. Otherwise, call for volunteers until everyone has had a turn being blindfolded.

4. Emphasize the idea of gentleness when the blindfolded child touches another. Younger children may be unintentionally rough. Watch carefully and guide the child if necessary.

5. If the blindfolded child has difficulty identifying the child in the circle, ask the child to say a few words to provide a clue.

Want to do more?

To make the activity more difficult, ask the children to extend their hands gently toward the blindfolded person. See if she can guess a child's name just by touching hands. • Or reverse roles by asking all those in the circle to close their eyes. Choose someone to go into the center. This child can open her eyes. Ask those in the circle to join hands and walk slowly around. Now when the circle stops at "Still water," the child in the center will touch a child in the circle, who will have to guess her name.

Involving parents

Parents can set up two kitchen chairs closely facing each other. One child sits in a chair and closes her eyes. Another family member then sits in the opposite chair. The child touches the other person's face and tries to guess her name. If only one family member besides the child is at home, wait for an extended family gathering.

4⁺

My Friend

If there is an odd number of children, join the activity yourself to create two groups of equal size. You will need at least fourteen children for this activity.

What to do

1. Divide the children into two groups of equal size. One group joins hands and stretches to make their circle as wide as possible. The second group goes to the center and forms a second circle, facing the first.

2. When the music starts, the children in the outer circle begin to rotate in one direction while the children in the center close their eyes. When the music stops, the children in the outer circle stop and drop their hands. The children in the inner circle open their eyes, drop their hands and run to stand in front of the person facing them in the outer circle. Each child should have only one partner.

3. As soon as partners are determined, ask each child from the inner circle to name the child facing him, quickly, one after the other.

4. When the music starts again, children who were in the outer circle go to the center, while those who were in the center turn to face inward, join hands and begin circling around the others.

Want to do more?

Try switching the roles of the two circles. The inner and outer circles can both face the center and rotate in opposite directions. When the music stops, the children in the outer circle can stand behind those in the inner circle. The children in the inner circle would not immediately know who was going to name them. • Read *No Friends* by James Stevenson (Greenwillow, 1986).

Involving parents

Parents can involve their children in a family guessing game. A parent can begin by thinking of someone in the family and giving the child a clue, for example, "I am thinking of someone who really loves spaghetti." Keep giving clues until the child guesses correctly.

People words to use

names
gentle
group
equal
class

Center

Circle time

Things you will need

- Music

Knock, Knock

People words to use

names
group
class
home
visitor

Center

Circle time

Things you will need

• Two chairs

If you have more than fourteen children, you may not have time to give everyone a turn. If you play the game several times over consecutive days, everyone will have an opportunity to participate.

What to do

1. Arrange the chairs front to back. The front chair is "home," and the back chair is "the visitor."

2. Ask the children to sit together behind the chairs. Ask a volunteer to sit in the home chair and remain facing straight ahead, away from the other children.

3. After the volunteer is seated, point to one of the children, who will quietly take the visitor chair. After being seated, this second child should knock on the home child's chair while saying, "Knock, knock!" The child at home answers, without turning around, "Who's there?" The second child says:

   Listen real well, now you can't see.
   Listen to my voice and then guess me.

4. The child at home names the visitor without turning around. The visitor then goes to the home chair, and another volunteer becomes the visitor.

5. Continue until all the children have been named.

Want to do more?

For added difficulty, have two visitors talking in unison. How about three or four? Can the home child name each visitor? • Read *The Perfect Spot* by Robert J. Blake (Philomel, 1992).

Involving parents

Repeat the family activity suggested in "Still Water." This time, however, the blindfolded child tries to guess the other's name by listening to her talk. Encourage the family member who is talking to disguise her voice.

Hand Pictures

4⁺

This activity allows you to focus on the dramatic implications of movement as part of conversation. Hands can be as expressive as puppets.

What to do

1. Tell the children that their hands and fingers can tell stories or convey ideas without the use of words. Ask them, for example, to watch what your hands and fingers do and then guess which animals you were pretending them to be.

2. Take your hand and arm and make a snake motion along the floor. Can they guess that your hand is a snake? Try portraying with one hand a rabbit, a bird, a spider, a fish. Can they guess each one correctly?

3. Ask the children to act out an animal with one hand. Can the other children guess the animal being portrayed?

4. Increase the difficulty by asking them to watch your hands and guess what action is happening.

   You are climbing a tall tree.
   You are eating something.
   You are catching a ball.
   There are waves along a river.
   The rain is falling softly (or quickly).
   The sun has come out.

5. Ask for a volunteer to act out something for the others to identify. Encourage the children to guess. Take turns with them.

Want to do more?

To increase the difficulty, put on the following brief plays, moving your hands as though they were puppets.

Two people are arguing, then fighting.
Two people have decided to become friends. They approach each other and hug.
One person feels sad, the other afraid.
One person knocks on a door; the other answers and says hello.

• To decrease the difficulty, give the children answers to choose between. You might, for example, ask, "Is this a snake or a bird?"

Involving parents

Parents can play a similar game with their children at home.

People words to use

stories
conversation
hands
fingers
guess

Center

Circle time

Things you will need

• Nothing

The Magic Pocket

Communication means translating an idea into a form—words or gestures—that can be understood by others. Giving life to ideas through communication is critical to social life, whether we are making friends or resolving conflicts.

People words to use

stories
communication

Center

Circle time

Things you will need

• Nothing

What to do

1. Tell the children you are going to pretend to take something out of a magic pocket. You will also pretend to use it. When you are done, you would like to see if they can guess what you took out of the pocket.

2. Take each of the following objects out of your magic pocket and engage in the suggested action. Each time, invite the children to name the imaginary object.

   hammer a nail
   throw a ball
   peel a banana
   eat a sandwich
   saw wood
   cut paper with scissors
   drink from a glass

3. Ask the children to take turns finding something in their magic pockets to show others in the class. Can other children guess what these objects are?

Want to do more?

Make whatever is in your magic pocket more elaborate. Take out several items with which to set a dinner table or play a game. Try unfolding objects to form much larger items like an automobile or rowboat.

Involving parents

Provide parents with instructions for playing "The Magic Pocket" with their children.

My Family

4+

Draw your own family to begin the activity. Children who cannot obtain photographs of their families will feel less left out if your picture is similar to theirs. Whenever an activity requires resources from home, plan ahead of time how to involve those children whose parents cannot or will not contribute.

What to do

1. Contact parents directly or send notes home requesting photographs of everyone in each child's family, either individual or group pictures. Children who cannot obtain photos may draw pictures of their family members.

2. Tape the pictures to a bulletin board or wall in clusters so that each child's family is distinct. After all the pictures are displayed, talk with the children about family size, number of brothers and sisters, age differences and so on. "Who has a grandma living at their home?" "Who is an only child?" are a few of the questions you may ask. Emphasize that there are many different kinds of families.

3. Discuss the special contributions that each individual can make in her family. Try to convey the idea that children contribute to their family's well-being, for example, by giving older members an opportunity to feel proud about their ability to teach and care for someone younger.

4. Discuss the important functions of families. For example, you may ask, "Why is your family important to you?" "What would it be like if you didn't have a family?" "Did you ever miss your family when you had to stay with someone else?"

Want to do more?

Family portraits (see "Involving parents") can be placed together on a bulletin board. • Read *Families Are Funny* by Nan Hunt, illustrated by Deborah Niland (Orchard Books, 1992).

Involving parents

All the family members can draw their self-portraits on one large sheet of paper to make a single family portrait.

People words to use

class
group
belonging
family
special

Center

Circle time

Things you will need

- Photographs of each child's family
- Bulletin board space

Missing Person

People words to use

class
group
belonging
absent
identify

Center

Circle time

Things you will need

- One large bed sheet

Lightly placing your hand on the "mystery child" who is under the sheet will reassure her. You may also say to her, "Oh, mystery child, I am right next to you." Children should not be pressured to participate.

What to do

1. Gather the children in a circle. Briefly discuss the idea that even though people may sometimes disagree, everyone in the group is important. When someone is absent, he will be missed. Go around the circle and identify each person by name. If someone is missing from the circle, can anyone remember his name?

2. Tell the children that you would like them to try an activity in which someone in the group will hide. The rest of the group will try to guess who is missing.

3. Take out the bed sheet. Tell the children that you will first ask them to close (or cover) their eyes, then you will go around the inside of the circle and tap someone on the shoulder. That person should open his eyes and silently crawl under the sheet in the center of the circle. Explain that after the volunteer gets under the sheet, you will ask the children to open their eyes and guess who the missing person is.

4. Begin the activity by crawling under the sheet yourself and allowing the children to identify you as the missing person. Then return to the circle and ask a child to take a turn. Encourage children who are self-confident and likely to feel comfortable under the sheet.

5. If no one in the group can identify him, ask the child under the sheet to say something. The children can use this clue to help them guess.

6. Make sure several children have a turn.

Want to do more?

If the group is small enough, try reversing the rules. All the children get under the sheet and close their eyes. Tap one child on the head to leave the "tent." The remaining children have to guess who has left. Or increase the difficulty by choosing more than one child to be under the sheet or outside the tent. • Read *One Frog Too Many* by Mercer and Marianna Meyer (Dial, 1985).

Belonging, cooperation

4⁺

Class Flag

Every child should be encouraged to participate. Leave space on the flag for children who are absent.

What to do

1. Stretch the sheet out on a large tabletop in the art area.

2. Paint your school's name at the top of this "flag." Sketch a sun in the center of the flag.

3. Invite the children to help you make the class flag. They can begin by filling in the sun. Draw outlines of their hands around the outer edge of the sun. One finger of each child's hand should slightly overlap with the next child's to form a circle or semicircle around the sun.

4. Write the children's names under their hands.

5. Staple the flag to the pole and hang it inside the classroom or outside the front door.

Want to do more?

Ask the group to name things that children like to do at their school. Select four activities that are among the most liked. Draw a large circle on the flag and divide it into four equal sections. Ask the children to draw one of the favorite activities in each section. • Take the flag with you on class walks, the children taking turns being flag bearer. • Read *Let's Be Enemies* by Janice May Udry, illustrated by Maurice Sendak (Harper and Row, 1961).

Involving parents

Parents and children can make a similar "Family Flag" at home.

People words to use

class
group
belonging
flag
together

Center

Art area

Things you will need

- Fabric paint
- Paintbrushes
- Sheet approximately 3' x 4'
- Markers
- Pole about 6' long
- Stapler

4+

Penelope's Present

People words to use

class
group
belonging
story
taking turns

Center

Circle time

Things you will need

- Nothing

In this activity, the story is accompanied by sound effects. As you tell the story, make additional comments to fill in the time as the sound effects are repeated around the circle.

What to do

1. Seat the children in a circle. Talk a few minutes with them about taking turns. To illustrate, ask the children to say their names around the circle, one at a time, beginning with the child to your right (point). When everyone has had a turn around the circle, ask them to repeat a sound you will make with your hands. Begin rubbing your hands together. As the sound goes around the circle, ask the children to keep making that sound until you start a new sound that will also go around the circle. When the sound comes back to you, begin softly clapping your hands. The children should continue to rub their hands together until the clapping comes around to them. Do not try the rest of this activity until the children understand the idea of picking up and repeating a sound passed around their circle.

2. Once the children understand the directions, place both your hands quietly in your lap. Begin telling the story when everyone has stopped clapping. Feel free to add to or revise the story as you wish.

Once upon a time, Penelope Pig was so happy to be invited to Briarbutton the Rabbit's birthday party. She worked and worked and sewed a pretty new dress to wear. On the day of Briarbutton's birthday, she picked up Briarbutton's wrapped present (carrot stew, his favorite) and left with plenty of time because she had far to walk. Now as she walked along, the wind began to blow...(Begin rubbing your hands together.)

Oh, oh. Penelope looked up at the sky. "Looks like it might rain," she thought. She wrapped her arms tightly around Briarbutton's present and kept on walking. (Continue with the story until the sound comes back to you. Then begin snapping your fingers on both hands.)

Oh, no! Here comes the rain. Penelope began to walk even faster now. "I don't want Briarbutton's present or my dress to get all wet," she said. "Oh rain, please stop." (Continue until the sound returns to you. Then begin softly clapping your hands.) But the rain fell even harder and harder and harder. Penelope's dress began to get wet...and her present to Briarbutton got soggier and soggier...when Aristotle the Mouse arrived with an umbrella and held it over Penelope so she wouldn't get so wet. (When the sound returns to you, begin snapping your fingers again.)

The hard rain stopped and changed to softly falling rain. "Looks like the rain might stop," Aristotle said as they walked along the forest path to Briarbutton's house. (When the sound returns, begin rubbing your hands together.)

And gradually the rain began to stop and all you could hear was the wind and a few raindrops. Aristotle and Penelope finally arrived at Briarbutton's house. (When the sound returns, place your hands quietly in your lap.)

Even the wind began slowly to calm down...until everything was quiet. Penelope rang the bell. "Ding-dong!" When Briarbutton came to the door, Penelope and Aristotle said, "HAPPY BIRTHDAY!" Even though the box was kind of soggy, Briarbutton loved the carrot stew Penelope brought him. Everyone sure had fun at his party. *The End.*

Want to do more?

Make up a different story from another character's point of view. • Invite the children to make up a story with sounds. • Create different sound effects with your hands to illustrate simple stories. • Read *The Windchild* by Cheryl Harness (Henry Holt, 1991).

Involving parents

Send home a description of this activity for parents to try with their children. A rainstorm might be especially fun at a family reunion.

Whose Shoes?

People words to use

names
group
class
guess
belong

Center

Circle time

Things you will need

• Large paper bag

Consider making a few incorrect guesses to draw attention to children who are not being named.

What to do

1. Right before circle time, ask the children to remove their shoes and bring them to you. Ask them to gather for circle time. While they are settling down, place one shoe from each pair in a large paper bag. Bring the bag with you to the group.

2. Tell the children that you are going to play a guessing game with them. Inside the bag is one shoe from each child in the group. You are going to take the shoes out of the bag, line them up and ask the children to guess who owns each shoe. Emphasize that they should not say if the shoe belongs to them.

3. Make a row of the shoes, telling the children not to start guessing until you ask them to.

4. Begin with the shoe at one end. For each shoe, ask, "Now who do you think belongs to this shoe? Can you name this person in our group?" Remind the children not to say anything about their own shoes until you have gone through the entire row of shoes.

5. After the children guess the owner for each shoe, return to the first one in the row. For each shoe, say something like, "Now, some of you thought this shoe belonged to _____; some of you said it belonged to _____. Let's see who the real owner is." Ask the child who owns the shoe to claim it.

6. When the game is finished, the children put their shoes (both of them!) back on.

Want to do more?

Children can bring toys from home in a paper bag without showing any to their classmates. Line the toys up in a row and see who can guess who brought each toy.

Involving parents

One family member sits at the kitchen table with her eyes closed. Another family member places an object in her hands. After feeling the object, she tries to guess who brought it.

Come Over

4⁺

Leaving and then joining a group that is in constant change reflects the type of informal group membership experienced by young children. Children are less likely to be overlooked if adults are present to provide guidance for both lines. Encourage children to choose someone who has not yet been named from the other line.

What to do

1. Form the children into two lines of equal length facing each other about 15 feet apart.

2. Huddle one line together and ask someone to identify a child in the other line. Once this child is named, then begin the chant:

   Red Rover, Red Rover, let _____ come over!

   The named child leaves his group to join the group that called him.

3. The other line now has a turn to select someone to join them. The sequence is repeated until all the children have been named.

Want to do more?

To make the activity more challenging, each child can be asked to "come over" in a different way. For example:

"Red Rover, Red Rover, let _____ skip over!" Or "Red Rover, Red Rover, let _____ walk backwards over!"

Involving parents

Parents can help their children make a telephone call to a distant faily member. Letters can be substituted for calls.

People words to use

names
group
class

Center

Movement area

Things you will need

- Nothing

Guess What Happened!

People words to use

stories
conversation
life

Center

Circle time

Things you will need

- Nothing

Life is a drama, and a story is at the heart of every satisfying conversation. In this activity, you will use your entire body instead of just your hands to communicate dramatically.

What to do

1. Prepare five pantomimes of familiar situations for children.

   Someone picking at her food, showing her dislike of it and rocking slightly as she holds her tummy.

   Someone picking flowers, smelling them and putting them into a vase.

   Someone fluffing up a pillow and falling asleep.

   Someone picking up, then feeding a baby.

   Someone taking a banana from a basket, then peeling and eating it.

2. Call the children together for circle time. Tell them you are going to act out something a person might do. When you are done, you want them to guess what happened.

3. Act out the pantomime and ask the children to guess the circumstances.

4. When you are finished with what you prepared, invite the children to take turns pantomiming something which the group will try to interpret.

Want to do more?

Increase the difficulty of the activity by pantomiming more complex situations. Instead of pantomiming while you sit, get up and use more space and physical action. Open doors and windows, climb ladders, play a game of catch, row a boat or perform other familiar activities.
- Explain to the children the type of activity and ask them to guess further details. For example, "I'm going to pretend to eat something. See if you can guess what I'm eating." Pantomime eating a banana. After the children guess what you are eating, pantomime eating an orange, then a lollipop, then a bowl of cereal.

Involving parents

Describe the activity to parents. Suggest they introduce it as a game for the entire family. Emphasize that actions selected by adults and older children should be as simple as possible to keep a young child involved.

4⁺

Name Pantomime

Shy children may find it difficult to be the center of attention. Children who hesitate or act bashful can perform their action while remaining in the circle.

What to do

1. Ask the children to stand, holding hands in a large circle. Tell them you have a "name game" for them to try. Someone will start by going into the center of the circle and saying:

   Hello there, how do you do?
   My name is _____
   So watch what I do.

   At that point the person makes a simple motion with her body. For example, she might begin by saying the chant and then waving her arms like a bird. Then everyone responds with:

   Hello _____,
   We'll do it too!

   Then the entire group copies what the first person did.

2. Begin the activity by volunteering to demonstrate. Make a distinct motion with your hands, body or feet after giving your name. You can make a circle with your arms, clap your hands or turn around in place.

3. Emphasize to the children that you want them to do something that other people can copy.

Want to do more?

To make the activity more difficult, volunteers can combine movements made by two or more parts of the body—like clapping while turning in space. Even more complicated actions, like dance steps, can be tried.
• Read *Hansel and Gretel* retold by Rika Lesser, illustrated by Paul O. Zelinsky (Putnam, 1989).

Involving parents

Parents can try the same activity at home, copying each other's actions.

People words to use

names
group
class
volunteer
copy

Center

Circle time

Things you will need

• Nothing

Our Rising Stars

People words to use

class
group
belonging
unique

Center

Circle time
Art area

Things you will need

- Several rolls of ribbon, each a different color
- Stars cut from construction paper, one for each person in the class
- Crayons
- Stapler or tape
- Scissors
- Display area (large bulletin board, wall, etc.)

Each child works separately to create something that is combined with the individual creations of others to form one single group display.

What to do

1. Write your name or draw your picture on one of the stars.

2. Bring the star and ribbons to circle time. Ask the children what they know about "stars" and "comets." Discuss for a few moments.

3. Teach them the following poem:

   Stars up in the sky so bright
   Glimmer in the dark of night.
   Each of us is like a star
   Shining brightly near and far.

4. Tell the children you would like to make a display in which each of them will have their own special star. Dismiss them to the art area.

5. Give each child a precut star. Ask them to draw a picture of themselves on their star and decorate it as they desire. Each child can also cut two or three short lengths of ribbon to attach with tape or staple to the bottom of the star.

6. When each child is finished, attach the stars to the bulletin board or wall. Cluster them together as a group.

7. After all the stars are attached in the display, gather the children near the bulletin board and discuss what they have done. Emphasize that every star is different, yet they all fill the sky together. Every star is special, just like every child in the group is special. Repeat the poem together.

Want to do more?

If you do not want to cut the stars ahead of time, draw them first on a sheet of butcher paper and ask the children to fill them in. • Read *Peter's Song* by Carol P. Saul, illustrated by Diane deGroat (Simon and Schuster, 1992).

Involving parents

Send home precut stars and ribbon for parents to create a "family stars" display with their children.

Family Show and Tell

4⁺

When a child brings his container of belongings from home, make sure to label them carefully and store them safely until he leaves for home. When other children interrupt with comments about their family, gently return the focus to the child who brought the belongings. These interruptions are acceptable as long as the child whose turn it is retains the spotlight.

What to do

1. Schedule each child in your group for a "family show and tell" at the beginning of the first circle time for the day.

2. Ask the parents of the child whose turn is approaching to gather something special from each member of their family for their child to bring to school as part of "family show and tell." (See "Involving parents.")

3. When your first circle time begins, ask the child to remove the objects from the container, one at a time, and tell the rest of the group who in his family likes the object and why it is special for that person. Ask the other children if someone in their family likes something similar.

Want to do more?

Family members can be asked to choose objects from a specific category, like clothes or entertainment. Pictures of the child's family can be placed on a bulletin board near the circle time location. • Read *Big-mama's* by Donald Crews (Greenwillow, 1991).

Involving parents

Ask parents to provide their child with a special object from each family member to bring to school for a "family show and tell." These objects should be placed in a sturdy container. They should not be too valuable, though, in case the container is dropped. Ask them to take a few minutes to explain to their child why each person likes the objects selected.

People words to use

family
belongings
show and tell
like
preferences

Center

Circle time

Things you will need

• Nothing

The Class Gallery

People words to use

class
group
belonging
unique
special
identical
portrait

Center

Art area
Circle time

Things you will need

- One long sheet of butcher paper
- Crayons
- Tape or stapler
- Display area

Making every circle the same size and shape establishes a common basis for belonging in the group. Personal decoration will emphasize individuality within the group.

What to do

1. Draw a row of identical large circles across the length of the paper, one for each teacher and child in the group.

2. Invite the children to visit the art area and draw a self-portrait in one circle. Demonstrate by drawing a portrait of yourself in a circle.

3. Write each child's name underneath his portrait.

4. The children may decorate the sheet with other drawings as long as the portraits remain clearly visible.

5. Tape the gallery to a wall or staple it to a bulletin board.

6. Conduct a circle time near the gallery. Point out the similarities and differences among portraits. Some may have blond hair, others brown or black. Some or all the faces may be smiling. Invite the children to comment on what they see. Emphasize the uniqueness of each child in the group.

Want to do more?

The children can draw their portraits on separate sheets of construction paper instead of on one long sheet. Be sensitive to different family structures and situations. • Also leave space at either end of the sheet for children who may join your group later in the year. Adding their portraits is an excellent way to greet and involve a new child in the group.

Involving parents

Send home a section of butcher paper and a description of this activity to help parents and children make a "family gallery."

Mystery Person

5+

In this version of "Is It Bigger than a Bread Box?" children have to depend exclusively on verbal clues for guessing a mystery person's identity. Knowing something about another is an important part of friendship.

What to do

1. Tell the children that you are thinking about someone in the group and that you would like them to guess who it is. You have some clues to help them guess.

2. Select yourself as the first person to be guessed. Begin with a common characteristic and gradually become more specific. The children raise their hands when they think they know who it is. If, for example, the author began with himself, he might say something like, "This person likes to play with puppets...this person likes fairy tales...this person is a teacher...this person is tall and has a beard...this person is bald."

3. Continue with clues about one of the children in the group.

4. After several rounds of guessing, invite one of the children to select someone and give clues.

Want to do more?

To increase the level of difficulty, give activity clues such as "someone who likes to play in the sandbox," or abstract clues such as "someone who has two brothers and two sisters." • Read *Julius, The Baby of the World* by Kevin Henkes (Greenwillow, 1990).

Involving parents

Parents can try a similar activity at home, including extended family members known to their children as possible "mystery persons."

People words to use

individual
familiar
guess
clues

Center

Circle time

Things you will need

- Nothing

Mystery Voices

People words to use

names
group
class
voice
guess

Center

Circle time
Art area

Things you will need

• Tape recorder

By gradually increasing the difficulty of the activity, you will provide a challenge that keeps children involved without becoming frustrated.

What to do

1. Ask children to come individually to a quiet location where you will record their voice. Ask each child and teacher in the classroom to make the same statement, such as "I like you" or "Do you know what my name is?"

2. After everyone's voice has been taped, play the tape during circle time and ask the children to identify who is speaking. Play the tape at another time for children who may be reluctant to guess in a large group.

Want to do more?

Leave the tape and tape recorder at a table with a set of photos for the children to match with the voices.
• Increase the difficulty by asking the children to make a vocal sound only, like "hmmmm" or "ohhhh." Then progress to one short word. Pause for a moment, then ask the child to make a longer statement.

Involving parents

If parents have access to a tape recorder, the entire family can play a game of "Mystery Voices." The children can bring the school tape home, play it for their parents and identify the voices.

Whose Hands?

Be sure to get the store owner's permission before assembling children to use the photocopier. Close the cover when making the picture and clean the glass when you are finished.

What to do

1. Take the group to a photocopier and photocopy one of each child's hands. Sequence the copying in alphabetical order to help in identification. Record the names in pencil on the back of each picture. Do not let the children see the copies at this time.

2. When the children gather for circle time, show them the stack of photocopies. Tell them you are going to go through the stack, one at a time, to see if the children can guess whose hand is pictured.

3. Show each hand, one at a time, and invite the children to guess to whom it belongs. Do not tell them whether they are right or wrong. ("So you think this is Jamie's hand? Let's go through them all and then we will find out.")

4. After completing the first round, review the set of pictures again, this time identifying whose hand is pictured.

5. At the end of the activity, pin all the hands on a bulletin board and identify them with the children's names.

Want to do more?

Polaroid pictures of hands are fast and convenient. • You can tape a "gallery" of hands on a classroom wall or bulletin board. • Photocopied hands can also be cut out and pasted together on butcher paper. • Read *Baby Hugs* by Dave Ross (Thomas Y. Crowell, 1987).

Involving parents

Family members can gather around a photocopier for a "group portrait" of their hands.

People words to use

names
group
class
copy
guess

Center

Circle time

Things you will need

- Photocopier
- Pencil

What You Wear

People words to use

individual
group
notice
details
important

Center

Circle time

Things you will need

- Nothing

This activity will give children an opportunity to do more than simply look at each other. To detect change, they will have to pay attention and really see the detail that makes up another person.

What to do

1. During circle time, briefly talk with the children about how important everyone, each individual person, is to the group. Being noticed by others helps individuals feel comfortable in the group. Tell the children that you have a "what you wear" game for them to play.

2. Stand up and ask the children to take a good look at you. After a few moments, ask them to wait while you make a change in how you look.

3. Leave the group (or ask them to close their eyes) and make a significant change in your appearance. For example, you can take off your shoes or eyeglasses or put on a hat. When you return, ask the children to guess what you have changed.

4. To make the activity more challenging, make more subtle changes, like switching your watch from one wrist to the other, untying a shoe or removing a small item of jewelry. Provide clues if the children cannot detect the change.

5. Invite the children to volunteer to be the center of attention. Suggest what to change or add if they seem uncertain what to do.

Want to do more?

Try changing facial expressions or body postures. • Read *Bently and Egg* by William Joyce (Harper Collins, 1992).

Involving parents

Describe the activity for parents to try at home.

My Mobile

5+

This activity focuses on self-awareness as well as on sharing and learning about each other. Draw other children's attention to the mobile created by one of their classmates as the day progresses.

What to do

1. Tell the children that each of them is going to create a collection of things to hang on a clothes hanger. This arrangement is called a "mobile."

2. Set out the magazines and art materials. Ask the children to find a picture of food they like to eat. When they finish, ask them to find a picture of a place they like. Continue with a person, an animal and, finally, a toy.

3. Cut out squares of construction paper for each child and ask them to draw small self-portraits.

4. Glue or paste the pictures to construction paper. Make holes at the top of all the pictures and self-portraits, string a piece of yarn through each of the holes. Hang each child's collection from a clothes hanger (younger children may need help).

5. Ask each child to bring her mobile to circle time. Go around the circle and ask the children to describe what they selected.

6. Hang all the mobiles in a central location. Point out differences and similarities among the children in the class.

Want to do more?

The children can simply browse through the magazines, selecting six things they like without specific categories in mind. • Make a mobile for yourself to show children in your group. • Read *Rosie and Michael* by Judith Viorst, illustrated by Lorna Tomie (Atheneum, 1974).

Involving parents

Show the parents their child's mobile. Describe the activity and suggest that each family member make her own "My Mobile" at home.

People words to use

like
food
person
animal
toy
sharing

Center

Art area
Circle time

Things you will need

- Plastic clothes hanger for each child
- Yarn cut in various lengths (7"-12") (about six lengths for each child)
- Several magazines with pictures of food, places, people, animals and toys
- Scissors
- Construction paper
- Glue

Getting to Know You

People words to use

class
group
belonging
information

Center

Circle time

Things you will need

• Tape recorder and tape

This activity may be the most difficult for many children because it relies exclusively on verbal rather than visual information about someone else. Remember, never pressure any child who hesitates to make a self-disclosure.

What to do

1. Over a period of several days or even weeks, in a quiet setting, tape an interview with each child in your group. The interview should be about five minutes in length. Ask such questions as:

   What is one of your favorite foods?

   What is one of your favorite toys?

   What is one of your special places to visit?

   Name something that gives you a sad (happy, angry or scared) feeling.

   Be sure not to mention the child's name in the interview. Once all the interviews are completed, select one to play for the group.

2. Call the children together for circle time and tell them you would like to play one interview. After the tape is played, ask the children to identify who was interviewed. Also go over the main points made in the interview. Emphasize that now the group knows more about the child than they did before. Ask the children to identify other important comments the child made.

3. Introduce the other interviews on other days, no more than one on any particular day. Contrast—do not judge—each interview with those previously played. Emphasize that differences of opinion and feeling are acceptable.

Want to do more?

During circle time, ask the children to recall information from a previous interview. • Read *The Owl and the Pussycat* by Edward Lear, illustrated by Jan Brett (Putnam, 1991).

Involving parents

Give parents the list of questions you are asking children before making the tapes. They can help prepare their children for the activity by discussing the topics with them.

Chapter Two

Compassion

Dear Parents,

Our second major goal for The Peaceful Classroom is compassion. Caring for oneself and others depends on remaining emotionally alive and responsive to the emotions of others. We hope to show children how to give words to the emotions of sorrow, anger, fear and joy. We want to help them understand that feelings are different from actions and that they can express their strong feelings in a positive way. We also want them to respond compassionately to the suffering of others.

Every person feels angry, frightened, sad at some time. Such feelings can often be frightening. The storm and fury of intense emotions can cloud our thinking. During those moments, we may feel out of control and at the very edge of danger. Managing the strong emotions that are a part of our humanity is one of the greatest challenges each of us has to face.

As they grow up, some people insulate themselves from these feelings. They view strong emotional experience as a form of weakness. Others may give in to the storm and allow themselves to be taken over by their emotions. They may feel powerless in the struggle to manage their passion. Some discover how to learn from their feelings and how to direct the energy of those emotions to bring them closer to others.

During the year we will use words like "happy," "sad," "angry" and "afraid" in our discussion with children. Children will participate in group activities like "Make a Face," "The Little Lonely Star" and "Emotion Tags." We will also be reading carefully selected picture books that focus on emotions and compassion. Each component of The Peaceful Classroom Program will be sensitive to the ages of the children involved. We will stay in touch with you about the program as it proceeds. We would also be interested in hearing any suggestions you might have.

Sincerely,

Emotions Picture File

Some children have no words to express how they feel. They need to hear such words as "happy," "sad," "angry" and "afraid" if they are to understand their emotional experiences. The "Emotions Picture File" is a basic tool you will need for many of the activities in this section. With younger children, begin with basic emotions and progress to complex emotions which are more difficult to understand.

What to do

1. *Activity 1*: During circle time, hold up one of the pictures and ask the children how this person feels. (If they do not know, tell them.) Ask the children to talk about what they see that makes them think the person feels that way. Point out facial expressions or other features which suggest the emotion.

2. *Activity 2:* Stack at least three pictures of each emotion on a table in your classroom. Mix up the order of the pictures. Hand the stack to a child and ask him to group all the sad pictures together, then all the happy ones and so on.

3. *Activity 3:* Either at a table or during circle time, show several pictures portraying the same emotion and ask the children to identify how all the people feel.

Want to do more?

You can show illustrations from children's books that visually represent emotions.

Involving parents

Urge parents to use simple words like "angry," "happy," "sad" and "frightened" as they talk with their children.

People words to use

Basic Emotions:
anger
sadness
fear/afraid
happy

Complex Emotions:
excitement
disgust
jealousy
courage
boredom
love

Center

Circle time

Things you will need

- A collection of pictures cut from magazines, each showing children or adults experiencing one of the emotions listed above. Glue to identical sizes of heavy construction paper or card stock. Number pictures on the back.
- Laminate.

How Do *You* Feel?

People words to use

Basic Emotions:
anger, sadness,
fear/afraid, happy

Complex Emotions:
excitement, disgust,
jealousy, courage,
boredom, love

Center

Circle time

Things you will need

A collection of pictures cut from magazines, each showing an **object** or **situation** that might trigger an emotional reaction in children. The pictures, however, should not show any obvious emotional reactions taking place. For example, your collection can include pictures of spilled ice cream, a broken tricycle or teddy bear, a spider, a dog, different amusement park rides, a skydiver, a delicious-looking dessert, a picture of a monster (for older preschoolers), a beautiful tree or garbage. The pictures should suggest a wide variety of emotional reactions. Glue to identical sizes of heavy construction paper or card stock. Number pictures on the back. Laminate.

"How Do **You** Feel?" pictures are a companion tool to the "Emotions Picture File." Instead of pictures of people experiencing emotion, the emphasis here is on situations that trigger different emotions.

What to do

1. *Activity 1:* During circle time, hold up one picture and ask the children how they would feel to be near the object or part of the event. Emphasize that people are sometimes different in how they feel about things. Some people are frightened of spiders, for example, others are not.

2. *Activity 2:* Ask the children to sort through the pictures with a specific emotion in mind. For example, they could look for things that make them feel angry. Then sort them into pictures that frighten them, pictures they like and pictures that make them sad. They can choose pictures more than once.

3. Make note of which pictures the children select.

Want to do more?

For younger children, tell the group how you might have felt as a child about what is pictured. • You can point to situations or objects illustrated in children's books. • Read *William's Doll* by Charlotte Zolotow, illustrated by William Pène du Bois (Harper and Row, 1972).

Involving parents

Ask parents to find pictures of something that they felt happy, sad, frightened or angry about as a child. They can use these pictures to engage their children in a discussion about emotions.

Make a Face

The ability to interpret body language, especially facial expressions, is a key to understanding the emotional experiences of others. "Reading" another person correctly is an important aspect of compassion. The face is a window to the human heart.

What to do

1. Show the children the cards, one by one, and ask if they know how each person feels. When finished, place the cards where all the children can see them.

2. Tell the children that you are going to pretend to feel like one of the people in the pictures and that you would like them to guess how you feel. Make a face that shows the emotion you chose. Repeat this several times for other pictures.

3. Continue with another round, emphasizing body language this time. For example, you might shake your fist and stomp your feet for anger. Reemphasize that you are pretending to have the feeling.

4. Let the children have the opportunity to demonstrate feelings by asking them to take turns choosing an emotion and making faces for the other children to interpret.

Want to do more?

With older children, choose three basic emotions. Ask for three volunteers. Whisper a different emotion to each child (or show them one of the pictures). Each child takes a turn, demonstrating the emotion through facial expression and body posture. The remaining children guess what emotion each of the three has demonstrated.

Involving parents

Parents can play a similar guessing game with their children. They can choose an emotion, make a face and ask their children to guess the emotion portrayed.

People words to use

Basic Emotions:
anger
sadness
fear/afraid
happy

Complex Emotions:
excitement
disgust
jealousy
courage
boredom

Center

Circle time

Things you will need

- One card from the "Emotions Picture File" portraying each of the emotions you want to discuss.

The Little Lonely Star

People words to use

lonely
sad

Center

Circle time

Things you will need

- One apple for every two children
- One knife

Storytelling can powerfully demonstrate how human beings affect each other emotionally. For example, a character may feel less sad after experiencing the sympathetic tenderness of another person. Understanding this cause-and-effect is a critical element in learning compassion and other forms of kindness.

What to do

1. Ask children if they know what it means to be "lonely." Discuss their ideas.

2. Tell them a story about the Little Lonely Star. (Keep the apples out of sight.) Elaborate on the plot as you wish. Use simple gestures to give added drama to the story.

   Once upon a time the sky was very dark at night. There were no stars...except one...a very tiny star. This little star was all alone and felt very lonely all by himself in the sky.

   One day this lonely little star went to see a very wise, very old, old man who lived on the earth on the top of a high mountain. The lonely little star asked the old man if he could help. Because the old man loved this little star very much, and because he was very wise, he said he would do two things.

   First, the old man reached behind him and pulled out a beautiful, shiny black bag. He opened it up, reached in and pulled out a handful of shimmering, glimmering stars. With one great swoop of his hand, he filled the night sky with a thousand stars.

   "There," said the wise old man. "Now you have many stars to be your friends. But because you have been so lonely, I am going to do something else for you. I am going to place you on earth, inside something special." He snapped his fingers, and it was done. *The End.*

3. Ask the children, "Do you know where the wise old man put that sad little star?" (Take out the apples.) "Why, inside every apple is a place for a tiny star. Watch, and let's find out if there really is something like a star inside this apple."

4. Cut the apple horizontally to make two equal portions. Pull the apple apart and show the "star" to the children. Cut the other apples in half and give a portion to each child.

Want to do more?

Make up other simple stories illustrating sadness, anger and fear, each showing a compassionate reaction by one of the characters. • Read *Stars for Sarah* by Ann Turner, illustrated by Mary Teichman (Harper Collins, 1991).

Children can go home and tell the story and demonstrate the surprise ending to their parents. Encourage parents to look for compassionate reactions to emotions expressed in the books they read to their children.

Expression, respect/encouragement

3+

Poor Little Sad Eyes

Children are often criticized for the way they express their emotions. "Stop crying right now!" a mother may insist. "Don't you talk to **me** like that!" a father demands. Criticizing how children express their feelings will not make those feelings disappear. Telling a child what not to do is inadequate. If we do not like a child's behavior, we have to show her what to do to manage her emotions.

What to do

1. Read and act out the following poem:

   Poor little boy with sad eyes, (point to eyes)
   See him now, how much he cries. (mimic crying, hands to eyes)
   He tries to stop with all his might, (clench teeth, grimace)
   He doesn't know (shake head)
   That tears are all right. (nod head "yes" while pointing to "tears")

2. Repeat the poem, with the children joining in both the words and actions.

3. Ask the children if they think it is okay for boys and daddies to cry. How about girls and mommies? Invite them to talk about a time when they were sad.

Want to do more?

Make up your own poems about anger, fear and happiness, emphasizing behavior that is acceptable.
• Read *Christmas Moon* by Denys Cazet (Bradbury Press, 1984).

Involving parents

If you have the opportunity to meet with the parents as a group, explore with them acceptable ways to express emotion, especially anger. Send home the poem for parents to read with their children. Encourage them to talk with their children about a time they cried.

People words to use

sad

Center

Circle time

Things you will need

• Nothing

Sad Teddy

People words to use

sad
angry
afraid
happy

Center

Circle time

Things you will need

- A soft, cuddly teddy bear

When we talk about strong emotions, we send children a message that these experiences are part of being human. We can also emphasize that we are able to learn ways to express these feelings that bring us together and help us understand each other. Honest tears are not a sign of weakness, but of love and strength.

What to do

1. Bring the teddy bear to school and introduce him to your children. You can ask the children to help you select a name for the teddy bear. Make up a past for the bear. Tell the children how he arrived at their school. Emphasize that this is a very special teddy bear who will talk about feeling sad, angry and afraid. Set very clear rules about playing with the bear (for example, no throwing, keep him indoors, keep him in the dress up area).

2. Later in the year, use Teddy when you want to help children who are emotionally upset. For example, a child may feel sad because of the death of a pet or relative. Bring Teddy to circle time. Begin the discussion with something like, "Let's pretend that Teddy is very sad today. What do you think happened to Teddy?" Encourage the children to describe what they think happened to Teddy. "Listen" to Teddy and then tell the children about what

has happened. You may want to start the story yourself with a statement similar to one of the following:

"I have to tell you Teddy is sad today because he lost something very special."

"Teddy is sad because a friend is moving to a different town."

"Teddy is afraid today because the big boys in his neighborhood want to hurt him."

"Teddy is angry because someone broke his truck."

3. Make Teddy's problem similar to that of the child whom you want to reach, but do not directly duplicate the circumstances. Avoid painfully harsh examples that may alarm more than enlighten. Children will benefit from this discussion by listening and offering their own thoughts, rather than by being made the center of attention as someone with a problem.

4. Ask for ideas that might help Teddy. Ask the children to tell Teddy how they think he should respond to his problem. Someone may want to give Teddy a hug. When you are through, thank the children for their ideas.

Want to do more?

Do not overuse this type of activity. Introduce it when you believe a discussion about emotions would be most helpful. Balance discussions of angry, frightened and sad feelings with more positive experiences like excitement: "Teddy is so excited. He's going to stay overnight at a friend's house for the first time." And happiness: "Teddy is so happy; his grandpa and grandma are coming to visit." • Read *First Flight* by David McPhail (Little, Brown, 1987).

Involving parents

Show Teddy to parents and encourage them to engage in similar discussions with one of the stuffed animals or puppets at home.

Happy/Sad Person

People words to use

happy
sad
feelings

Center

Circle time
Art area

Things you will need

- Cups
- Grass seed
- Potting soil
- Felt tip markers

We often use the word "make" when referring to the source of our emotions. We say, for example, " You **make** me so mad!" "Make" implies force and helplessness. We cannot be responsible for how we feel if we are **made** to feel some way. But emotions result from how we interpret what happens to us. We speak more accurately if we say, "**I feel** angry when you say those mean things to me!" By taking responsibility for our feelings, we begin to help children assume responsibility for theirs.

What to do

1. During circle time, briefly talk with the children about feeling happy and feeling sad. Emphasize that sometimes people feel happy and sometimes they feel sad. Invite them to make a Happy/Sad Person in the art area.

2. Give each child a cup. Bring out the felt tip markers and ask them to draw a happy face on one side of the cup and a sad face on the other.

3. Once the faces are drawn, help the children fill the cups with potting soil to about four-fifths of their capacity. Sprinkle grass seed in each cup and cover with a light layer of soil. Water slightly and place the cups in a row on a window sill that gets indirect sunlight. Let the children turn the cup to face whichever way they want.

4. When the grass grows, the children can cut the "hair" into a desired shape.

5. Ask the children what they think might have happened to make Mr. Sad so sad. Ask about Mr. Happy, too.

Want to do more?

Children could also make Happy/Angry or Calm/Scared People. • Read *The Man Who Kept His Heart in a Bucket* by Sonia Levitin, illustrated by Jerry Pinkney (Dial, 1991).

Involving parents

Invite parents and children to make their own Happy/Sad People at home.

Emotion Tags

4⁺

Sometimes we may be frightened of expressing emotions to young children. We are most vulnerable when we reveal how we feel. These moments are also opportunities for children to reach out compassionately to us. When I told Steven, a four year old in my class, that I felt sick and "yucky," he put his arm around me and suggested, "Now Dokker Smith, you go home and your mommy take care of you." Children who express feelings when distressed are more likely than more reserved children to help someone in trouble.

People words to use

anger
sadness
fear/afraid
happy

Center

Varies

Things you will need

- Five name tags, each with a drawing of a face that reflects either happiness, anger, sadness, fear or disgust. (See the illustration.) These small pictures can be laminated and hole punched at the top. Use a safety pin to wear the tag.

What to do

1. When you are feeling particularly happy, sad, angry or afraid, pin on the appropriate "Emotion Tag."

2. The tag will draw children's interest and provide opportunities to talk about the emotion you feel. Discuss your feelings if the children are interested. Use simple terms and describe issues familiar to young children. For example, "I feel sad because someone I really like does not like me anymore," communicates clearly what you feel to young children.

3. Change tags as your feelings change through the school day.

Want to do more?

Set out "Emotion Tags" for the children to wear. The children can draw or paint their own tags.
• Read *Night on Neighborhood Street* by Eloise Greenfield, illustrated by Jan Spivey Gilchrist (Dial, 1991). • Make a tag for "yucky."

Involving parents

A similar set of "Emotion Tags" can be worn by family members at home.

Expression, cooperation

Emotion Drawing

People words to use

happy
sad
angry
afraid

Center

Art area

Things you will need

- A large sheet of butcher paper
- A variety of creative arts materials (glue, construction paper, crayons, paint, etc.)

Creative activity provides many opportunities for expressing our feelings. Each of us has a strong urge to communicate our emotional experiences in some way to others, if not to ourselves. This activity emphasizes expression through creative action, rather than drawing a specific picture.

What to do

1. Set out the art materials and butcher paper. With your children's help, establish an emotion theme such as: "Okay, let's make a happy picture!" or "Let's make a sad picture."

2. Distribute the materials and encourage the children to work cooperatively. Avoid suggesting a specific setting for the drawing, such as a circus for "happy" drawings. Each child can contribute ideas to create a mural effect. Thank them for their cooperative effort.

3. When finished, tape the "Emotion Drawing" to a wall. Examine the picture with the children and talk about how they portrayed the same emotion in different ways.

Want to do more?

Play appropriate music while the children draw. • They can also make drawings on separate sheets to be hung together like a gallery.
• Read *Fall Is Here! I Love It!* by Elaine W. Good, illustrated by Susie Shenk Wenger (Good Books, 1990).

Involving parents

Parents and children can draw together, taking one emotion as a shared theme.

4+

We Half Feelings

We make assumptions about how someone else feels by observing them and finding evidence that suggests to us a certain emotion. Tears, however, can signify either happiness or sadness. Only when we combine tears with downcast eyes and a slumped body posture, are we fairly sure that the person is sad.

What to do

1. Cut a slit in the construction paper "cover" slightly longer than the width of the new pictures.

2. In the art area, invite the children to play a guessing game with the new pictures. Keeping the pictures hidden from view, slip them under the cover. Slide a small part of one picture through the slit. Ask the children to guess how the person pictured feels.
Expose slightly more of the picture and ask again. Gradually reveal the entire picture.

3. Hide a different picture under the cover and gradually expose it from the bottom up, pausing to allow the children to guess.

Want to do more?

Set out materials for the children to use with each other. • Instead of cutting a slit, cut holes varying in size from large to small in different sheets of construction paper. Cover the emotion picture with several sheets, their holes overlapping and the sheet with the smallest hole on top. Ask the children to guess how the person feels. Remove one sheet at a time, gradually revealing more of the picture.

Involving parents

Parents can play a similar guessing game at home with their children.

People words to use

emotion
happy
sad
angry
afraid

Center

Art area

Things you will need

• New pictures to add to the "Emotions Picture File" representing the basic emotions.
• A large piece of construction paper
• Scissors

Emotion Puppets

People words to use

compassion
happy
sad
angry
afraid

Center

Art area

Things you will need

- Small paper bags
- Marking pens
- Rubber cement
- Scissors
- Construction paper

Children like puppets because they can safely pretend to be someone else without fear of criticism. The ability to project oneself into another person is the basis for compassion.

What to do

1. Using a small paper bag, make a sample puppet whose face expresses one of the basic emotions.

2. Set materials on the table in the art area and invite the children to make their own happy, sad, angry or afraid puppets. Have the "Emotions Picture File" available to provide examples of facial expressions.

3. Talk about experiences you had growing up that relate to emotions the children have selected for their puppets.

4. The children can name their puppets and write the name on the bottom of the bag, with your help, if necessary.

5. Set up a room divider in the dress up area to make a stage where children can perform their own puppet shows.

Want to do more?

Create your own puppet family, each puppet expressing a different emotion. Use these puppets to put on brief skits for the group.

Involving parents

Children can bring home their puppets to show their parents. Parents and children can make additional puppets together.

Happy/Sad Sticks

Avoid giving children the impression that there is a "right" or "wrong" response to the situations you describe. It may seem obvious to you what response a situation will call forth, but other people's reactions are not so predictable. How will a child feel whose toy is broken by a playmate? Angry? Sad? Or both?

What to do

1. Distribute paper plates to the children in the art area. Ask them to draw a happy face on one plate and a sad face on the other.

2. Staple each paper plate to the top of a flat stick.

3. Ask the children to bring their Happy/Sad Sticks to circle time. Ask them to hold up and show you the happy stick. Repeat with the sad stick. Tell them that you would like to find out how they think people feel at different times.

4. Describe each of the following circumstances. When finished, ask the children, "How did this person feel? Happy or sad? Show me either your happy or your sad stick."

   This person loves ice cream. After supper his mommy surprised him with a chocolate ice cream desert.

   This person's daddy gave her a really nice, gentle hug.

   This person's favorite truck broke into lots of little pieces.

   When this person came home from school, his mommy told him his dog Woofles was sick.

5. Create additional examples based on experiences familiar to your children.

Want to do more?

Make Happy/Angry and Happy/Afraid Sticks. Repeat the activity with these emotions. • To make the activity more challenging, introduce sad/angry, angry/afraid situations. Emphasize with older children that when something happens, some people may feel sad, while others feel angry. • Ask the children to close their eyes and imagine the situation while you talk. They can open their eyes when it is time to make a choice. This prevents your own expression from suggesting a response. • Read *After-School Monster* by Marissa Moss (Lothrop, 1991).

Involving parents

Parents and children can make their own Happy/Sad Sticks at home. They can take turns describing a situation while the other chooses a response.

People words to use

reactions
happy
sad
angry
afraid

Center

Art area
Circle time

Things you will need

- Two short, flat sticks (available from paint or hardware stores for mixing paint) for each child
- Two small paper plates for each child
- Stapler
- A variety of creative arts materials (glue, construction paper, crayons, paint, etc.)

Contrasting Feelings

People words to use

Basic Emotions:
anger
sadness
fear/afraid
happy

Complex Emotions:
excitement
disgust
jealousy
courage
boredom
love

Center

Art area

Things you will need

- Emotions Picture File
- Large sheet of paper
- Marker

Every emotion is a natural outcome of what we believe is true. Feeling follows thought. There are no irrational emotions, only irrational beliefs. If we believe something is dangerous, even though it is not, we will feel afraid.

What to do

1. On a large sheet of paper draw a horizontal and a vertical line to divide the sheet into four equal parts. In three sections, place pictures from the Emotions Picture File that depict the same emotion. Place a picture depicting a much different feeling in the fourth section (see illustration).

2. Tell the children that three of the pictures go together because the people in the pictures feel the same way. One does not belong because that person feels different from the other three. Ask the children to point to the one that is different. Take the picture selected and ask, "How does this person feel?" After a child responds, group the three remaining pictures and ask, "How do these people feel?"

3. If the children cannot name the emotions, point to the group of three and say something like, "These people feel **sad**. See their faces, how their mouths are turned down. See the tears in their eyes. They feel **sad**. Now this person over here feels

happy. (Point to the fourth picture.) See the smile on her face. She feels **happy**."

4. Take note of those emotions that children cannot identify. Introduce these terms in ongoing conversations with them.

5. Repeat with other emotions. Make the session playful.

Want to do more?

Use "How Do **You** Feel About This?" pictures instead of the Emotions Picture File. Tell them that three pictures go together because many people are frightened of these things. The other is something usually considered less frightening. Keep in mind that these situations are potentially ambiguous. There is no right answer. Ask the children to describe the reasons for their choices. • Read *That's Good! That's Bad!* by Margery Cuyler, illustrated by David Catrow (Henry Holt, 1991).

Involving parents

While reading a book or magazine together, parents can ask their children how someone in a picture feels. If the child does not know, the parent can identify the feeling.

Face Plates

4+

Emotions like sadness, fear and anger are often identified as "bad" emotions. We say, "I feel bad," instead of "I feel sad" (or afraid, or angry). Such a negative evaluation is understandable given the amount of criticism we experience for being sad, angry or afraid. Avoid labeling any emotion so negatively.

What to do

1. Cut out a variety of construction paper eyes, eyebrows, noses and mouths that can be combined to reflect different feelings. Place these features in the art area with the paper plates, glue or paste, paint and crayons.

2. When the children arrive, ask them to identify which pieces are eyes, eyebrows, noses and mouths. Give the children paper plates and ask them to make faces using the pieces.

3. When they are finished, encourage them to identify the kind of feeling that the face they made shows—if they are interested in discussing it. The children can then decorate the faces with either crayons or paint and the collage materials.

4. Collect all the faces and tape them to a wall. Encourage the children to identify which faces look happy, sad, scared—or scary—and angry.

Want to do more?

Hold up one of the plates and ask the children to make a face that feels the same way. • Read *My Mama Says There Aren't Any Zombies, Ghosts, Vampires, Creatures, Demons, Monsters, Fiends, Goblins, or Things* by Judith Viorst, illustrated by Kay Chorao (Atheneum, 1973).

Involving parents

Parents and children can make face plates together at home.

People words to use

happy
sad
angry
afraid

Center

Art area

Things you will need

- Construction paper
- Scissors
- Small paper plates
- Collage materials (yarn, bits of material and paper, etc.)
- Glue or paste
- Crayons or paint

I'm Happy Sometimes

People words to use

happy
excited

Center

Circle time

Things you will need

• Nothing

Happiness is the reaction we have when we believe we have experienced good fortune. Happiness provides the energy to move toward the attraction.

What to do

1. Ask the children to tell you what being "happy" means. Tell the children a true story about a time you felt happy when you were young. Describe an experience similar to something children in your group might have gone through. What **physical** feelings did you have? Were you smiling, trembling, your heart pounding? What was so attractive to you? What did you **do**?

2. Let the children take turns telling the group about a time when they felt happy.

3. Teach them the following poem:

   When I'm feeling happy, (smile)
   The world is such a sight!
   (hand over eyes "looking")
   Hugs for you, hugs for me,
   (point to others, then hug self)
   Smiles as bright as sunlight.
   (hands outstretched)

4. Ask the group the following questions:

   What are some things that children feel happy about?

   What are some ways we can help others feel happy?

Want to do more?

Older children can draw a picture or write a story about a time when they were happy. • Read *Silly Fred* by Karen Wagner, illustrated by Normand Chartier (Macmillan, 1989).

Involving parents

Send the poem home for parents and children to learn together. Encourage parents to talk about some of their happy experiences growing up.

I'm Sad Sometimes

Sadness is the emotional reaction we have when we believe we have experienced a loss. We no longer have something precious to us. The child cries after losing his teddy bear or after the death of a pet. Mourning means coming to terms with the loss and recreating a self without the loved person or thing.

What to do

1. Ask the children to tell you what being "sad" means. Tell the children a true story about a time you felt sad when you were young. Describe an experience similar to something children in your group might have gone through. What **physical** experience did you have? Were you nauseous, trembling, crying? Did your heart feel "heavy?" What was the **loss** you thought you had? What did you **do**?

2. Let the children take turns telling the group about a time when they felt sad.

3. Teach them the following poem:

   When I'm feeling sad, (make a sad face)
   Sometimes I have to cry. (run fingers down from eyes)
   I need a hug from mom or dad (hug self)
   And a tender lullaby. (grasp and rock arms)

4. Ask the group the following questions:

   What are some things that children feel sad about?

   What can we do when we feel sad?

5. Talk with the children about ways to understand and manage what feels like a loss. Some alternatives include: getting adult help, talk

ing about the sadness, finding a substitute, helping someone else, learning a new skill. Make your suggestions relevant to the losses the children describe.

Want to do more?

Older children can draw a picture or write a story about a time when they were sad. • Read *I Don't Care* by Marjorie W. Sharmat, illustrated by Lillian Hoban (Dell, 1979).

Involving parents

Send the poem home for parents and children to learn together. Encourage parents to talk about sad moments they experienced growing up.

People words to use

sad
lonely
crying
grief
loss

Center

Circle time

Things you will need

- Nothing

I'm Afraid Sometimes

People words to use

fear
afraid
scary
nightmares
danger
courage

Center

Circle time

Things you will need

- Nothing

Fear is the emotional reaction we have when we believe we are threatened or endangered. Fear gives us the energy to flee or overcome the danger. See also "No Stranger To Danger."

What to do

1. Ask the children to tell you what being "frightened" means. Identify several words for fear. Tell the children a true story about a time you felt frightened when you were young. Describe an experience similar to something children in your group might have gone through. What **physical** experience did you have? Were you nauseous, trembling? Were your hands sweaty? Was your heart pounding? What was the **danger** you thought was present? What did you **do**?

2. Let the children take turns telling the group about a time when they felt frightened.

3. Teach them the following poem:

   When I'm feeling terrified,
   (make scared expression)
   The world seems so spooky. (look around)
   I want to find a place to hide—
   (hands over head)
   Maybe you could help me.
   (point to others)

4. Ask the group the following questions:

   What are some things that children feel frightened of?

   What can we do when we feel frightened?

5. Talk with the children about ways to understand, manage and overcome what might be dangerous. Some alternatives include: getting adult help, talking about the fear, learning about the fear, avoiding the scary thing, learning a new skill. Make your suggestions relevant to the fears the children describe.

Want to do more?

Older children can draw a picture or write a story about a time when they were frightened. • Read *My Brother John* by Kristine Church, illustrated by Kilmeny Niland Tambourine (William Morrow, 1991).

Involving parents

Send the poem home for parents and children to learn together. Encourage parents to talk about scary moments they experienced growing up.

4+

I'm Angry Sometimes

Anger is the emotional reaction we have when we believe we are faced with an obstacle that prevents us from reaching a goal. Anger provides us with the energy to overcome the frustration.

What to do

1. Ask the children to tell you what being "angry" means. Identify several words for anger. Tell the children a true story about a time you felt angry when you were young. Describe an experience similar to something children in your group might have gone through. What **physical** experience did you have? Were your teeth gritted, fists clenched, hands sweaty, face hot, heart pounding, body trembling? What was the **threat** you thought was present? What did you **do**?

2. Let the children take turns telling the group about a time when they felt angry.

3. Teach them the following poem:

   When I'm feeling angry,
   (make an angry face)
   My face feels boiling hot. (fan face)
   *I am **mad**, you see. (point to self)*
   A fight? Let's not! (fist to palm, then
   shake hands and head)

4. Ask the group the following questions:

   What are some things that children feel angry about?

   What can we do when we feel angry?

5. Talk with the children about ways to understand, manage and overcome obstacles or frustrations. Some alternatives include: getting adult help, solving the problem, avoiding the problem, talking about the anger, learning a new skill. Make your suggestions relevant to the anger the children describe.

Want to do more?

Older children can draw a picture or write a story about a time when they were angry. • Read *Grandma Gets Grumpy* by Anna Grossnickle Hines (Clarion, 1988).

Involving parents

Send the poem home for parents and children to learn together. Encourage parents to talk about angry moments they experienced growing up.

People words to use

anger
mad
frustrated

Center

Circle time

Things you will need

• Nothing

Emotion Dancing

People words to use

sad
angry
afraid
happy

Center

Movement area

Things you will need

- Samples of music, each about two minutes long, each conveying a distinctly different emotional tone. Classical music provides the broadest range of emotion, from fear to joy. The soundtrack to the movie "Fantasia" offers excellent examples of the type of music you need.
- One silk scarf (or substitute) for each child.

Emotion is energy. Maybe that is why it is called e-**motion**. The experience of emotion brings vitality and movement into our lives. Fear, for example, helps us flee from danger; sadness, to mourn a loss. To feel is to be alive.

What to do

1. Ask the children to listen to each sample of music. After each sample, ask them how they felt while the music played.

2. After you have played all the music, give each child a scarf. Invite the group to stand and dance together as the music is replayed. Ask them to dance according to how they feel about the music.

Want to do more?

Give the children their own musical instruments and ask them to play happy, sad, angry and scared music. • To introduce an element of cooperation, ask the children to hold a partner's hand and dance to the music together. • Or play music while the children paint, and ask them to paint to the music. • Read *The Bear Dance* by Chris Riddell (Simon and Schuster, 1990).

Involving parents

While listening with their children, parents can talk about how they feel while the music plays. Parents can also dance with their children to the music.

Feeling Face Masks

5+

Feelings are often confused with behavior. We treat some emotions with disdain because of the associations we make between feelings and behavior—anger with hitting, fear with running away, for example. But emotions are not "bad." Actions may be harmful and beliefs irrational, but emotions are a natural part of being human. As you respond to children's behavior, make statements like, "I know you feel angry, but I **cannot** allow you to hit Cindy. No hitting in our school."

What to do

1. Show all the materials to the children when they arrive at the art area. Suggest that they try to make masks with either happy, angry, sad or frightened faces. Help them make holes at eye level so that they can place the bags over their heads and see what they look like.

2. Hand out the paper bags and materials and encourage the children to draw their own "feeling faces." While the masks are being made, discuss various feelings, how they originate and their consequences.

3. Display the masks you made earlier if the children need help understanding what to do. Do not, however, use your masks as models for children to copy. Let them create their own.

4. When the children have finished, invite them to guess what kinds of feelings the others have drawn on their masks.

5. Under close supervision, invite the children to wear the masks and see what they look like in the mirror.

Want to do more?

Masks can also be made from large paper plates using a rubber band stapled to the side as a headband.

Involving parents

Parents and children can make "Feeling Face Masks" at home together. Never allow a child wear such a mask unattended.

People words to use

happy
sad
angry
afraid

Center

Art area

Things you will need

- One large paper bag for each child
- Four bags upon which are drawn either a happy, angry, sad or frightened face
- Mask materials (crayons, construction paper, yarn, paste or glue, etc.)
- Scissors
- Large mirror

The Sound of Feelings

People words to use

anger
sadness
fear
happy

Center

Circle time

Things you will need

- Tape recorder
- Cassette tape
- Emotions Picture File

Deprived of all visual cues in this activity, children may have difficulty making a choice. Focusing exclusively on sound will help them observe auditory as well as visual emotional cues.

What to do

1. Convey each of the basic emotions on tape through the tone and inflection of your voice. For example, repeat a statement like "Hello, there," giving it a different emotional inflection each time. Say it sadly, happily, angrily, fearfully. Repeat a different statement, changing the order of emotions. Repeat single words like "Yes." Then shift to a more ambiguous vocalization like a humming sound. Make the same sound each time, but with a different emotional emphasis.

2. During circle time, place four pictures from the Emotions Picture File representing happiness, sadness, anger and fear in a row. Play a segment from the tape. Stop and ask the children to identify how the person saying the tape feels. Tell the children the emotion you were trying to portray. Continue with other segments.

Want to do more?

Encourage the children to make various sounds with specific emotions in mind. The teacher and the other children can try to guess what the emotion is. • Consider placing children in back-to-back chairs to eliminate visual cues.

Involving parents

Parents can repeat the activity at home, taking turns with their children, making sounds and guessing the emotions.

5⁺

Emotion Stories

The most important and dramatic moments in our lives are characterized by strong feelings. In stories, shifts in emotions are critical to plot development.

What to do

1. Decide on a sequence of basic emotions for your story. In this example, the sequence is happy-sad-happy-afraid-angry-happy.

2. Invite the children to make up a story with you. Begin with:

   Once upon a time there was a young girl just your age. One day she felt **really** happy about something that happened to her. *What do you think happened?*

3. At this point, call on one of the children to identify what the girl was happy about. Elaborate on this point in the story and move to the next emotion in your sequence. For example:

   Yes, her mommy and daddy, the queen and king, gave her a beautiful puppy for her very own. The puppy had long brown hair and droopy ears. She named him Shnooze. Together the princess and Shnooze would...(describe what they did together). Then something **sad** happened to the princess. *What do you think happened?*

4. Repeat the procedure in 3, elaborating on a child's response and moving to the next emotion in your sequence until you are finished with the story.

5. Invite the children to draw pictures illustrating part of the story. Post them on the bulletin board.

Want to do more?

Record the story for later listening with illustrations drawn by children. • Choose a different sequence of emotions for another story.

Involving parents

Parents can repeat this storytelling activity at home, blending sequences of emotions into a story they create with their children.

People words to use

happy
sad
angry
afraid

Center

Circle time

Things you will need

- Paper
- Crayons

Whose Feeling?

People words to use

Basic Emotions:
anger
sadness
fear/afraid
happy

Complex Emotions:
excitement
disgust
jealousy
courage
boredom
love

Center

Circle time

Things you will need

- "How Do **You** Feel?" pictures
- Paper and pencil

During the late preschool years, children begin to grow away from egocentrism—defined as the inability to understand the point of view or feelings of another person when these differ from one's own. This activity prompts children to see others as unique people with their own ideas, reactions and feelings.

What to do

1. Select one of the basic emotions. Note the choices children made for that emotion during the "How Do **You** Feel?" activity. For example, Terry said the spider would frighten him, Tim said the thunderstorm and Sarah said the snake.

2. Call the children together for circle time. Invite them to play a guessing game about the things other children in the group feel afraid of (or angry, or happy or sad about). Tell them you are going to ask for a volunteer. You will show the group three pictures. One was selected earlier by the volunteer as something that is frightening to him.

3. Gather three pictures together: the one the volunteer chose as frightening (the spider) and two that he did not (the amusement park ride and ocean surf). Set the three pictures in a row and say something like, "One of these three things frightens Terry; the other two do not. Which one did Terry select?" Affirm each child's right to feel any emotion in whatever circumstance arouses it.

4. Ask for another volunteer and continue as before. Make sure to vary the order of the pictures from child to child.

Want to do more?

To make the activity easier, choose more divergent situations. In the previous example, you could combine pictures of ice cream, a pretty tree and the spider. To make the activity more difficult, choose pictures that suggest more similar circumstances, like a spider, snake and lion. • Read *Mama, Do You Love Me?* by Barbara M. Joosse, illustrated by Barbara Lavalee (Chronicle Books, 1991).

Involving parents

Parents can identify four things that frighten them, of which only one actually does. Children can guess which one really frightens their parents.

Emotion Picture Studio

5+

Keep in mind that emotions are often intermingled; they do not simply replace each other. The mother who sees her child run out into the street feels simultaneously frightened, angry and loving. At any moment, however, only one feeling will seem to predominate. Like most activities appropriate for older preschoolers, the success of this one builds on their experience with the preceding activities.

What to do

1. During circle time, tell the children you would like to take photographs of them showing different emotions. Ask them to make a sad face, then a happy face, then an angry face, then a frightened face. Invite them to visit with you at your "picture studio" near the art area.

2. The "Emotion Picture Studio" is a table with a small chair at which children can sit. Children visit the studio one at a time. Ensure as much privacy as possible.

3. Ask a volunteer to sit at the table. Place one of the pictures from the Emotions Picture File in front of the child and ask him to make a sad (or happy, or angry, or frightened) face, too. Take a picture of the child showing the emotion.

4. When all the children have had a turn, put all the pictures together. As they did with the pictures in the Emotions Picture File, children can sort the photos into categories of emotion. Photos can also be used as "flash cards" to teach children words for the basic emotions. Use only those cards that clearly show an emotion.

5. Photos can also be organized into categories of emotion and displayed on a classroom wall or bulletin board.

Want to do more?

Exchange photos with another class and see whether children can guess the emotions portrayed.

Involving parents

Children and parents can draw pictures of each other reacting emotionally to different situations.

People words to use

anger
sadness
fear
happy

Center

Circle time
Art area

Things you will need

- Camera (a Polaroid is great)
- Film

Really Feelings

People words to use

sad
angry
afraid
calm
pretend

Center

Circle time

Things you will need

- Draw happy, sad, angry, calm and frightened faces on separate sheets of paper.

The idea that people sometimes act and appear one way while actually feeling another is difficult for five year olds to understand. Most preschoolers have not yet learned the subtle art of masking how they feel. But the rituals of emotional suppression are learned during the preschool years. For example, in a class of four year olds, I once asked Stephen how he felt as he was crying. Between sobs, he told me, "I feel **fine**."

What to do

1. Introduce the activity by saying something like, "Sometimes people do not want others to know how they really feel, so they put on a pretend face. They want to hide their feelings from others. Let's say you called me a mean name. I could smile and say, 'Now, you shouldn't say that.' (Pick up the happy face and then put it down.) But even though I have a smile on my face, deep inside I feel sad because I don't like to be called names." While talking, slide the sad face under the happy face.

2. Use the following stories to illustrate your point. Keep the second picture hidden from view until the end of each story.

   STORY 1: (Hide the sad face behind the happy one.) "This teacher broke a favorite dish when he was at home. Just then, a neighbor knocked on the door. When he answered the door, this is how the teacher looked (show happy face). *How do you think he really felt?"*

After a discussion, reveal the sad face. Explain that the teacher felt very sad because his favorite dish was broken.

STORY 2: (Hide the angry face behind the calm one.) "There was another time when a teacher had to tell a little boy in her class that he could not do something. The little boy became very mean and spit on the teacher. The teacher tried to remain calm. She told him he was not supposed to do that (show calm face). *How do you think he really felt?"*

After a discussion, reveal the angry face. Tell the children that the teacher was angry because she disliked being spit on.

STORY 3: (Hide the afraid face behind the angry one.) "There was another time when another teacher was outside watching children in his class play. One child climbed up on the very tall slide and began to jump up and down. The teacher saw this child almost fall off. He ran over to the slide, looked up at the child and told her to get down immediately. This is the way the teacher looked (show the angry face). *How do you think he really felt?"*

After a discussion, reveal the afraid face. Explain that the teacher was afraid because he knew that this child was in danger of being hurt.

Want to do more?

Invite the children to make up similar stories of their own.
• Read *The Moose in the Dress* by Bruce Balan, illustrated by Denise Teasdale (Potter, 1991).

Involving parents

Parents can talk with children about times when they have not wanted to show how they feel.

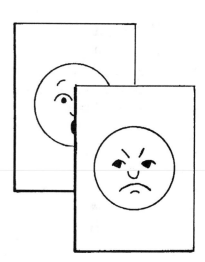

Chapter Three

Cooperation

Dear Parents,

Our third major goal for The Peaceful Classroom Program is cooperation. The ability to work together to achieve common goals is an important personal skill. We will encourage children to be aware of goals they have in common with others, to work together to achieve those goals and how to resolve conflicts nonviolently.

Children who have high self-esteem have a prosocial or collaborative view of personal power. They are willing to work with, not against, others. They do not have to prove their competence by dominating others through force or deception. They do not have to prove their excellence to themselves or others by winning. Their striving for improvement is based more on achieving personal or group goals than comparing themselves to others.

Instead of "building character," competition introduced by adults is more likely to heighten a child's fear of failure, invite comparison with others and diminish self-esteem. In contrast, cooperative activities enhance children's feelings of personal power and contribute to their sense of group belonging. Competition builds walls between people; cooperation builds bridges.

We will use words like "problem," "goal" and "cooperation" in our discussions with children. Children will participate in group activities like "Juicy Group," "We're All Winners" and "Cookie Machine." We will also be reading carefully selected picture books that focus on cooperation and conflict resolution. Each component of The Peaceful Classroom Program will be sensitive to the ages of the children involved. We will stay in touch with you about the program as it proceeds. We would also be interested in hearing any concerns or suggestions you might have.

Sincerely,

Mouse on the Run

3+

Cooperation first appears in young children when they give, take and return playthings to adults. This exchange has definite rules. The child offers the adult a toy to take and then expects it to be returned immediately. Through this type of involvement, children learn how to cooperate with others.

What to do

1. Arrange the children in a fairly tight circle. Take out the ball and say something like, "Oh, look. I'm going to pretend this ball is a mouse. Hello, little mouse. (Put your ear to the ball and pretend to listen.) He wants to walk around our circle. He's tired, so he wants to run real slow. So let's work together, cooperate, to pass the mouse around the circle. I will start. Okay, little mouse, here we go."

2. Give the ball to the child on your right and ask her to pass the "mouse" to the next person. Keep instructing the children until the mouse goes around the circle one full time without a problem. Then say, "Okay, mouse, stop! Now he wants to go a little faster. Let's see if you can make him go a little faster."

3. Once the children understand how to take and pass the ball, you can ask them to speed up or slow down to add variety.

Want to do more?

To increase the difficulty, add another ball. Try passing it in a different direction. • Play music of varying tempos to suggest slow or fast movement.

Involving parents

Now might be a good time to visit with parents to let them know about your emphasis on cooperation.

People words to use

cooperate
partner

Center

Circle time

Things you will need

- One soft, small ball

Dough It Together

People words to use

cooperate

Center

Art area

Things you will need

- 3 cups flour
- 3/4 cup salt
- Powdered tempera paint
- 1/2 cup of water
- Large bowl
- (Increase proportionally in order to make enough for all the children.)

Cooperation means **pooling** resources with others to accomplish a task. Young children are capable of cooperation. Anna Freud observed nineteen-month-old toddlers taking turns while building a tower of blocks.

What to do

1. Divide all materials (flour, salt, water, tempera paint) into small portions.

2. Tell the children you would like them to make some playdough. They will have to work together, cooperate, at the table to succeed. Give a small portion of one of the ingredients to each child at the table. Encourage all the children to become involved in the preparation. (For example, one child adds the water to the bowl, the next mixes in the flour, the next adds the salt, etc.) The group can pass the bowl around to take turns kneading the dough.

3. When finished, the group can divide the dough into portions for each child sitting at the table. Following a period of play, return the playdough to a container designated for the group and refrigerate for later use.

Want to do more?

Other activities can be divided into tasks given to individuals within a work group. For example, prepare a salad by giving each child a specific responsibility. One child can cut or tear the lettuce, another peel the carrots, another cut the carrots (with supervision), another open and drain a can of kidney beans, etc.
• Read *Clap Your Hands* by Lorinda Bryan Cauley (Putnam, 1992).

Involving parents

Send home the playdough recipe for parents to make with their children. Provide a small amount of powdered tempera paint, if possible.

Double the Fun (or How to Find a Partner)

Many activities for children involve working in groups of two. Left free to pick their own partner, children who tend to be exclusive in their choices will limit their opportunities to relate to others. Here are two methods that use chance to form partnerships among children.

What to do

1. Untangling yarn: Arrange the lengths of yarn side by side. Gather the ends so that they protrude about four inches from your hand. Ask each child to select one end from one string of yarn. When you let go, challenge the children to unravel the strings without letting go of the end in their hand. Can they find their partner at the other end of the string?

2. Matching shapes and colors: Take each pair of construction paper shapes and shuffle them with all the other pairs. Distribute one cutout to each child. When all are distributed, ask the children to find the one that matches theirs. This person will be their partner.

3. If there is an odd number of children, join in the activity. If not, help where needed.

Want to do more?

To make the yarn activity more difficult, overlap the lengths back and forth before the children try to unravel the yarn. • Matching shapes can be made more difficult by reducing the number of colors and making the shapes more complex or more similar.

Involving parents

Many of the activities you suggest to parents involve children and adults working together as partners. "Double the Fun" could be tried at home as a fun way to find a partner.

People words to use

partner
cooperate

Center

Varies

Things you will need

- 4' lengths of yarn, all the same color, one length for each pair of children
- Pairs of identical (in shape and color) construction paper cutouts, one pair for each pair of children

Juicy Group

People words to use

cooperate
goal
together

Center

Circle time

Things you will need

- One orange for each teacher and child
- One small bowl for each child
- Pitcher
- Paper cups
- Knife
- Small cutting board
- Spoon (to remove seeds from bowls)
- Napkins
- Washcloth and towels

Every child needs to feel powerful. We can help children learn to channel their personal strength to create harmony rather than disunity and conflict. Loss of power, the inability to make things happen or to make a difference—these are the roots of violence.

What to do

1. Ask the children to wash their hands thoroughly before beginning.

2. Take out your orange and hold it up for the children to see. Take a minute to talk about what they know about oranges. Cut a thin slice from the orange. Pass it around and ask the children to hold it up to the light so that they can see the beautiful design of the fibers. Can they smell the orange?

3. Pass out the bowls and napkins. Tell the children you are going to see how well they can cooperate to make a pitcher of fresh orange juice. Take your orange and slowly squeeze the juice into a bowl. Hold up the bowl so the children can see the juice.

4. Cut each orange into quarters. Hand a segment to each child and ask him to squeeze the juice into the bowl. When the children finish, ask them to pour their juice into the pitcher and begin squeezing another quarter. Comment on how each child's effort contributes to the common goal.

5. When through, pass out the cups and pour each child some juice. Talk about how they all worked together.

Want to do more?

Use an old-fashioned glass orange juicer after the children are finished squeezing to extract all possible juice from the orange quarters. Let them eat the remaining pulp from the quarters when they are through making juice. • Read *Lots to Do* by John Prater (Ideals, 1991).

Involving parents

Encourage parents and children to work together to make their own orange juice at home.

3+

Butter Lover

Although adults may have to impose turn-taking rules in group activities, young children do spontaneously take turns in the games they create on their own. This cooperation helps to establish the order and harmony that makes group play possible.

What to do

1. Pour the cream into the jar and pass it around the circle, encouraging the children to take turns looking at and smelling the contents. When the container returns to you, salt the cream lightly, cover the jar tightly and shake vigorously.

2. Pass the container around and encourage the children to shake it vigorously, too. (You may have to take several additional turns yourself.) Once the cream thickens into butter, spread it on crackers or bread and give to the children for a snack.

3. Emphasize the idea that everyone worked together and cooperated to make the butter. Discuss how it tastes.

Want to do more?

Music can be played to enhance the rhythm of shaking. • Try the butter on different kinds of bread or crackers. • Bring in sticks of butter to compare to what the group made. • Read *Garage Song* by Sarah Wilson, illustrated by Bernie Karlin (Simon and Schuster, 1991).

Involving parents

Children can show their parents how to make butter at home. Family members can take turns shaking the butter jar.

People words to use

cooperation
taking turns
together

Center

Circle time

Things you will need

- Whipping cream
- Salt
- Bread or crackers
- Large jar with secure top

We're All Winners

People words to use

cooperate
balance
support

Center

Movement area

Things you will need

- Small area rug or other safe surface where children can gather
- Or chalk for drawing outdoors on cement

Competition is encouraged when children are taught by adults that games must have winners and losers. No child loses in the activities in this book. No one is isolated or rejected because they failed. The responsibility for reaching a goal is shared by the group.

What to do

1. Tell the children you would like to see how well they can cooperate. Lay the rug in the center of the circle and ask the children to pretend that it is an island. They are swimmers who need to reach the island. They will have to work together, cooperate, to see how many of their group will fit on the island.

2. Ask the children to move to one end of the room. Then ask them to begin swimming to the island. Count the children as they reach the rug. Emphasize that no part of their bodies should touch the "water" once they are on the island.

3. Fold the rug in half and repeat the activity.

4. Roll the rug into a tube and repeat the activity. Balance and support now become more important as the children work together to fit as many as possible on the available space. Supervise closely.

Want to do more?

Cardboard boxes can serve as boats. Increase the surface area to make the activity easier; decrease to make it more difficult. • Read *Muddigush* by Kimberly Knutson (Macmillan, 1992).

Involving parents

Families can try to squeeze together on rugs of different sizes or inside cardboard boxes.

3+

Class Nature Collage

In some families, parental pride is contingent upon the child's distinguishing herself in comparison to others. Parents promote competition when they compare their children to one another.

What to do

1. Tell the children you would like them to work together to make a class collage of pretty things found outside. Explain what it is and is not permissible to take. Permissible objects include leaves fallen off trees, pebbles or things thrown away by people like bottle tops or tin foil. Anything that is alive or belongs to someone else should not be taken.

2. During outside play, give the children about ten minutes to find something they think is pretty or interesting.

3. Back inside, ask the children to bring what they found to circle time. Set the posterboard in the center of the circle and ask each child to place her contribution somewhere on the board. When everyone is finished, ask if they would like to change the position of their contribution.

4. When the collage is ready, glue or tape the objects to the board for later display.

Want to do more?

Instead of gluing or taping, find a spot where the collage can be seen but not disturbed. Let the children make a freestanding arrangement to be admired over the next several days. • Read *On Our Way to Market* by Dayle Ann Dodds, illustrated by John Gurney (Simon and Schuster, 1991).

Involving parents

Parents and children can make their own nature collage together at home.

People words to use

cooperate
together
contribution

Center

Outside
Circle time

Things you will need

- Posterboard
- Glue or tape
- Crayons

3⁺

Hand Me Pictures

People words to use

cooperation
contribution
everyone
group
together

Center

Circle time

Things you will need

- A sheet of paper and crayon for each person in the group
- Tape

Terry Orlick, pioneer in cooperative games, found that, from preschool to second grade, children who experience cooperative games are three to four times more likely to play cooperatively on their own. Children without this experience become more competitive as the years progress.

What to do

1. This activity gives children an opportunity to contribute and to receive a picture created by the entire group.

2. Give each child several crayons and a sheet of paper with his name at the top. Tell the children that they have a short time to draw whatever they want on their paper.

3. After about one minute, ask the children to pass the paper to the person on their left (demonstrate). Ask the children to add to the drawing in front of them. As the pictures circulate, the children contribute to each one.

4. Stop when the drawings return to their originators. Each child now has a drawing composed of the work of everyone in the group.

5. Talk about how they all worked together to create the drawings. Tape all the pictures together on a wall.

Want to do more?

Ask smaller groups to sit around tables in the art area. Provide additional art materials (paint, glue, collage material, etc.) for the children to use in making pictures passed around the table.

Involving parents

Children and parents can complete "Hand Me Pictures" at home.

3+

Group Soup

Terry Orlick found that children reported feeling happier when playing games based more on cooperation than competition. If given a choice, children prefer cooperation.

What to do

1. A few days before actually cooking the soup, talk with the children during circle time about the many ingredients that can go into a "group soup." Ask for volunteers to bring such vegetables as carrots, potatoes, celery, tomatoes, onions and cabbage. Just about any vegetable can be added to the list. You contribute the chicken or beef bouillon.

2. Send notes home with the children requesting that the foods be brought to school on the day or day before you make the soup. Request that all food be fresh rather than canned or frozen.

3. When the children arrive on the cooking day, ask them to bring their food to circle time. (Bring a few potatoes or carrots for children who forgot their food.) Take a piece of each food and circulate it around the group. Do not allow the children to eat the food. Encourage them to get a feeling for the texture, appearance and odors of each vegetable.

4. After examining the vegetables, the children should wash their hands and meet at the tables to prepare the food.

5. Supervise all food preparation. Peeling and cutting utensils can hurt. Take the time to show the children how to prepare the food safely. Rinse the food after it is prepared and immediately put it into the pot or plastic bags for later use. Add bouillon and water to the soup pot.

6. While the soup is cooking under close supervision, the children can continue with other classroom activities. Vegetable cooking times vary, so you may want to start some items before adding others. When the soup is finally cooked and served, compliment children on their cooperation in making the group soup.

Want to do more?

You can prepare some of the food and allow the children to finish. For example, cut three-fourths of the way through the carrots and let the children finish the cut with a less dangerous butter knife. • Read *Stone Soup* by Tony Ross (Dial, 1987).

Involving parents

Parents can take their children shopping for vegetables, then involve them in the preparation of soup at home.

People words to use

cooperate
contribute
prepare
group

Center

Circle time
Kitchen area

Things you will need

- Kitchen utensils and a pot for the preparation and cooking of soup
- Food brought by children and teachers
- Salt and pepper for seasoning
- Soup bowls and spoons
- Hot plate, if no stove is available

3+

Tug of Peace

People words to use

cooperate
together
effort
group
individual
accomplish
task

Center

Outside

Things you will need

- One rope about 3/4" to 1" thick, approximately 40'-50' long
- A very heavy, but moveable object (large wooden crate, piece of plywood holding a stack of bricks, small boulder, log, etc.)
- Gloves for children (brought from home)

Never compare a child's performance to another's to motivate her to do better. Her focus should be on setting and achieving a worthy goal, instead of doing better than someone else.

What to do

1. Gather the children around you and tell them you have an activity that will require them to work together to move something heavy.

2. Tie the rope securely around the heavy object so that two equal lengths of rope remain. The object should be heavy enough that the group can successfully move it only with great effort. The rope should be strong enough to withstand the strain.

3. Divide the children into two equal groups and assign each group to one end of the rope. Ask them to put on their gloves. On command, both groups begin to pull the rope and try to move the object to a reasonable distance designated by the teacher. Supervise them closely for safety.

4. Do not hesitate to become involved. Shout words of encouragement and praise as the children pull. When finished, discuss the merits of cooperation to accomplish a difficult task. Point out—and let anyone who wants to, try—that no single individual can move the object alone. Only a group can do it.

Want to do more?

Have a "Tug of Peace" between the teacher(s) and children. Eight or nine determined preschoolers make a good match for a relatively strong adult. You may be surprised how strong a group of young children can be when they work together.

Involving parents

Ask parents to set up several situations in which they and their children work together to achieve a goal. For example, children and parents can lift and move a heavy box together. Parents should involve their children cooperatively even though they are capable of achieving the goal alone.

4⁺

Rockabye

Rockabye, like many activities in this book, has two distinct objectives. The children doing the rocking cooperate to offer kindness to another. The child being rocked is the recipient of both their cooperation and their kindness.

What to do

1. Stretch out the blanket and ask the group to form a circle. Talk for a few minutes about gentleness and cooperation.

2. Ask for volunteers to take a "Rockabye" ride. The volunteer lies down on his back in the center of the blanket.

3. The rest of the group stands and lifts opposite edges of the blanket, slightly raising the child off the ground.

4. Once this is accomplished, invite the volunteer to close his eyes. Begin swinging the blanket gently back and forth. Compliment the children on their cooperation.

5. After about a minute, lower the volunteer gently to the floor and repeat with another child.

Want to do more?

Distribute adults equally around the blanket to help out with support. • Consider playing peaceful, happy music while the child is rocked. • Read *The First Dog* by Jan Brett (Harcourt Brace Jovanovich, 1988).

Involving parents

Parents and other family members can work together to "Rockabye" one of their young children.

People words to use

cooperate
gentle
kindness
volunteer

Center

Circle time

Things you will need

- Sturdy large blanket or sheet
- Music

4+

Cookie Machine

People words to use

cooperate
volunteer

Center

Movement area

Things you will need

- Small, sturdy area rug

Parents will probably find it difficult to emphasize cooperation with their children in a society that glorifies competition. Some parents may justify placing their children in competitive situations in order to prepare them for the eventual reality of winning and losing. Young children, however, first need a history of cooperation to prepare them to cope with the pressures of competition.

What to do

1. Invite the children to cooperate to make an imaginary "cookie machine." Ask for one volunteer to be the cookie and two volunteers to be chefs.

2. Ask the remaining children to sit in two equal lines about 3' apart. They represent the ingredients. Place the rug at one end between the lines. Ask the "cookie" what kind of cookie—oatmeal, raisin, chocolate chip—she would like to be. Ask the cookie to lie on her back on the rug.

3. When the cookie and the chefs are ready, and each part of the machine knows what ingredient they are to contribute, then begin. For example, some children will put in the flour, some the sugar, others the raisins and chocolate chips. The final four children can be the oven, joining hands over the cookie and humming as it "bakes."

4. Ask the chefs to pull the rug holding the cookie between the lines to the other end, where it will be baked. Offer help if needed.

5. Repeat with another volunteer. If you have enough children, you can have two cookies on the production line, one after the other.

Want to do more?

Make other kinds of food, too. How about a salad?

Involving parents

Families can set up their own "cookie machines," "salad bars" or "car assembly lines" on a double bed or living room floor. The "cookie" can roll instead of being pulled from one part of the "machine" to another.

Balloon Bounce

4+

Children who work cooperatively are more likely to encourage others and see them as partners instead of competitors. Children who are not locked in competition are more willing to help each other.

What to do

1. Ask the children to stand and make a circle. Tell them that you have a game to play that will require working together—cooperating. You will toss a balloon into the air, and their goal is to keep it in the air without touching the ground. You will count how many times the group hits the balloon. After a child hits the balloon once, she has to go back to her place and let someone else have a turn.

2. After returning to their place in the circle, their job is to remain there and to hit the balloon back into the center of the circle if it comes their way. Once everyone has had a turn, and the balloon has not touched the ground, the group has won. Emphasize that they should hit the balloon gently upwards into the center of the circle to make it easier for others to hit.

3. Go to the center of the circle and ask the children to gather around you. Then toss the balloon straight up into the air. Remind the children to go back to the circle after hitting the ball.

4. After the last child has had a turn, or the balloon touches the ground, begin again and encourage the group to better its previous score.

Want to do more?

Lay a rope along the floor to provide a boundary. Divide the children into two groups and ask the groups to move to opposite sides of the rope. Ask the groups to bounce the balloon back and forth across the boundary without letting it strike the ground. Count the number of hits the children make. When the balloon strikes the ground, start over and encourage them to beat their previous score. • Read *The Ornery Morning* by Patricia Brennan Demuth, illustrated by Craig McFarland Brown (Dutton, 1991).

Involving parents

Parents and children can repeat the activity at home.

People words to use

cooperate
gentle
encourage
together

Center

Circle time

Things you will need

• One balloon

Puzzles for Us

People words to use

cooperate
together
group

Center

Circle time

Things you will need

- Different colors of construction paper
- Scissors
- Envelopes

Children who experience the value of cooperation are more likely to work cooperatively in the future.

What to do

1. Make simple puzzles by cutting sheets of construction paper into three different pieces (see the illustration). Place each set in an envelope.

2. Divide the children into groups of three. When they are ready, tell them you have a puzzle for them to solve. Each child will get one or more pieces, and together they will have to solve the puzzle.

3. Give each group an envelope. Tell them that each envelope has puzzle pieces in it that together form a rectangle. Ask each child to take a piece of the puzzle from the envelope. When everyone has a piece, ask them to put their puzzle together. Encourage their efforts and give hints where necessary.

4. When a group completes a puzzle, give them a more difficult one to do.

5. When you are finished with the activity, talk about how well they worked together, cooperated, to solve the puzzle problems.

Want to do more?

Make the activity more difficult by increasing the number of pieces and making each piece less distinctive (see the illustration). • Make the task easier by cutting the sheets into two pieces and asking the children to form partnerships instead of groups of three. • Let the children make puzzles for others to solve. • Read *Family Farm* by Thomas Locker (Dial, 1988).

Involving parents

Parents can purchase or make simple puzzles appropriate to their child's age and assemble them together.

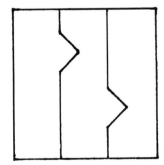

Balloon Pick-Up

4⁺

Increased competition distracts children from experiencing the pleasure of accomplishment. They become more preoccupied with the performance of others.

What to do

1. Blow up all the balloons and put them where they will not drift around the room (e.g., in a corner behind some chairs).

2. Divide the children into groups of three. Reconvene for circle time and ask the groups of three to sit next to each other.

3. Tell the group that you would like to see how well they can cooperate. Each group of three will try to get as many balloons as they can off the ground before the timer buzzes. One child will be the "balloon stuffer" while the other two hold balloons between their heads, hands, tummies, legs, etc. The balloon stuffer becomes a balloon holder after the other two are holding as many balloons as they can.

4. Set the timer for about two to three minutes. Begin the timer and count each balloon held off the ground. Cheer the threesome on. When time runs out, or they have held as many as they can, another group will take a turn.

Want to do more?

For added challenge, blindfold the two holders. Now the stuffer has to give more direction to the holders. • Decrease or increase the time to change the difficulty level. • Read *Will You Please Feed Our Cat?* by James Stevenson (Greenwillow, 1987).

Involving parents

Parents and children can do the activity together at home.

People words to use

cooperate
group

Center

Circle time

Things you will need

- About 25 balloons
- Kitchen timer

Back Stand

People words to use

cooperate
partner
interlocked
together
effort

Center

Movement area

Things you will need

- Nothing

A competitive environment increases tension and frustration and can trigger aggressive behavior among the winners as well as the losers.

What to do

1. Ask the children to form partnerships. Tell them that you would like to see how well they can cooperate. Ask partners to sit back-to-back. When they are ready, ask them to stretch out and interlock their arms with their partner's. You will probably have to demonstrate this.

2. When their arms are interlocked, ask them to work together to stand without letting go of their partner's arms.

3. When the children are finished, ask them to sit facing each other with their legs slightly bent and their feet touching. They should then take hold of each other's hands. Can they pull each other up to a standing position?

4. Encourage the children in their efforts. Comment on their attempts to cooperate.

Want to do more?

Try having three or four children sit back-to-back and stand with their arms interlocked. Ask these larger groups to sit facing each other, take the hands of two others in the group, and lift each other to a standing position.

Involving parents

Parents and children can try passing an egg to each other from one teaspoon to another.

Basket Catch-It

4⁺

Set up conditions you believe to be challenging but not too frustrating. Allow children to change the rules to adjust the game to the most enjoyable level of difficulty. Inflexible rules are the hallmark of competitive games. Such rules place more skilled children at an advantage.

What to do

1. Tell the children you would like to give them an opportunity to work together and cooperate. Ask them to choose partners.

2. When everyone has a partner, form two lines with partners facing each other. Give each child a basket. Hand the beanbags to the children in one line. Tell the partners they will have to work together to throw the beanbag and catch it in the baskets. They can set their basket on the ground when it is their turn to throw.

3. After five to ten minutes of throwing and catching, ask the children to meet in circle time. Talk with them about how well they worked together.

Want to do more?

Change the difficulty of the game by increasing or decreasing the size of the basket or the distance between partners. • Read *Amos and Boris* by William Steig (Puffin Books, 1977).

Involving parents

Parents can try "Basket Catch-It" at home.

People words to use

cooperate
together
partner
line

Center

Movement area

Things you will need

- One small basket for each child
- One beanbag for every two children

Body Drawing

People words to use

cooperate
generosity
partner
volunteer
outline
gallery

Center

Art area

Things you will need

- Sheets of butcher paper about a child's height in length
- Crayons
- Paint
- Collage material
- Glue
- Chalk (if outside)

Competition undermines generosity. People focused on winning are not likely to give to their competitors. Cooperation strengthens generosity because achievement becomes a shared goal.

What to do

1. Ask the children to choose a partner. Give each pair a sheet of butcher paper. Set the art material on a nearby table.

2. Tell the children they will have to cooperate to complete this art activity. They are going to help each other draw pictures of their bodies. Ask them to decide who will go first.

3. The volunteer lies down on the sheet of paper, and the partner draws around the contour of her body to create an outline.

4. When the outline is finished, both children work together to add detail where desired with the art material. Tape the completed drawings on a classroom wall to form a class gallery.

5. Give the pair another sheet of butcher paper and repeat the activity with the other partner.

Want to do more?

Work in teams of three instead of two. • Make a class gallery using different colors of chalk on the sidewalk in front of your school.

Involving parents

Send home long sheets of butcher paper for parents and children to use working together to make "Body Drawings."

Stick Together

Children in our culture learn that winning requires conflict. Someone has to lose. In most cases, there is only one winner. Under these conditions, even winning becomes uncomfortable and unsatisfying. With cooperation, everyone can achieve.

What to do

1. Divide the children into groups of two.

2. Ask the children to pretend that their bodies are really sticky. What would happen if different parts of their bodies actually stuck together? What would that be like?

3. Begin playing the music. "Okay, partners, let's see your hands stick together...now your toes are stuck together." (Follow with knees, ankles, elbows, etc.) After a few commands, ask them to switch partners. Encourage the children to be gentle in their contact.

4. After several rounds, sit down to relax and discuss how well everyone cooperated.

Want to do more?

Ask partners to maintain contact while moving around, if possible.
• Ask partners to join with other partners to make a group of four.
• Read *Farm Morning* by David McPhail (Harcourt Brace Jovanovich, 1985).

Involving parents

Parents and children can play "Stick Together" at home.

People words to use

cooperate
gentle
win
lose
group
partner

Center

Movement area

Things you will need

• Record turntable or tape player
• Lively music

Two Islands

People words to use

cooperate

Center

Circle time
Movement area

Things you will need

- Two medium-sized area rugs
- Two 1" x 6" boards about 5' long

Under no circumstances should the boards be raised more than a few inches. Because of the increased risk of falling, closely supervise any activity requiring balance.

What to do

1. Tell children the following story:

   Once upon a time there were two islands. One island had a lot of trees and pretty rivers; the other had beautiful mountains and rich green valleys. After a while, though, the people living on these islands became tired of seeing only what was around them. They wanted to see the pretty things on the other island. But there was no bridge, and it was too far to swim. *How could they solve their problem?*

2. Place the two rugs about nine feet apart. Divide the children equally between both islands. Once everyone is on an island, set a board down on each island.

3. Tell the children you would like to see if everyone from one island can get to the other without falling into the "water." Anyone who touches the "water" will have to return to their island to start over.

4. Encourage the children as they proceed. There may be more ways to solve the problem than the obvious.

Want to do more?

Give the children a rope and see whether that suggests additional strategies. • For an interesting challenge (a good place to start with five year olds), create three islands, a far island about 9 feet away from a middle island, and a near island about 14 feet away. Each gets a 5' length of board. The goal is to get children on the near and far islands to switch places. • Add more islands of different distances, each with a different length of board. • Read *The Bear's Water Picnic* by John Yeoman and Quenton Blake (Atheneum, 1987).

Involving parents

Parents and children can try "Two Islands" at home, using rolled up rugs for logs if boards are not available.

Bubbles in a Basket

4⁺

Encouragement is sometimes difficult to distinguish from pressure. What we thought was encouragement could turn out to have been pressure, if we react to a child's failure with disappointment or hostility.

What to do

1. Divide children into groups of four. Tell them you would like to see how well each group can cooperate. Each group will have a turn trying to blow a bubble across the room so that one of the partners can catch it in a basket.

2. Lay the rope across the floor in a line to form a boundary at one end of the room. Choose one team to go first. One child takes the container and goes behind the boundary. Position the other three partners at the opposite end of the room.

3. Set the timer for about two to three minutes. Blow a few bubbles well up in the air near the group. Encourage them to work together to blow one of these bubbles across the room to their waiting partner before the timer goes off.

4. If the bubble breaks, then make another one for them at that spot.

5. When the timer goes off, give the next group in line a turn.

Want to do more?

Place the rope in a circle. The catcher cannot leave the circle.
• You may increase or decrease the size of the container to make the activity easier or more difficult. • Increase the number of children in a group to make it easier. • Give the children a piece of construction paper to use as a fan if they get tired of blowing.

Involving parents

Parents and children can cooperate with a game of "Bubbles in a Basket" at home.

People words to use

cooperate
encourage
group
partner
line

Center

Movement area

Things you will need

- Bubble solution and blower
- 6' length of rope
- Small lightweight container (like a plastic bowl)
- Timer

Cat and Bird

People words to use

cooperate
group
together
circle

Center

Circle time

Things you will need

- Three balls, two of the same color, one of another color

This variation of mouse-on-the-run adds an element of complexity. Two goals, escape and capture, are simultaneously pursued by the group.

What to do

1. Arrange the children in a fairly tight circle. Take out the ball that does not match the others and say something like, "Pretend this ball is a bird. Hello, little bird. (Put your ear to the ball and pretend to listen.) She wants to walk around our circle. She's tired so she wants to walk real slow. So let's work together, cooperate, to pass the bird around the circle. I will start. Okay, little bird, here we go."

2. Give the ball to the child on your right and ask her to pass the "bird" to the next person. Keep instructing the children until the bird goes around the circle one full time without a problem. Then say, "Okay, bird, stop! Now she wants to fly across the circle. Whenever I say 'stop and fly', stop the bird and roll it across the circle to someone else. Let's try that now. Okay, bird, walk around the circle." Have the bird stop, fly and then walk several times so the children understand how to move the bird around and across the circle.

3. Stop the bird and hold up one of the two balls of the same color. Say, "Oh, no! Here is a cat. I will start the cat around the circle, too. If the cat catches the bird, what happens? Now the cat can only walk around the circle. You can

walk the bird around the circle or have it fly by rolling it to someone else. Let's see if the cat can catch the bird." Add the cat to the circle when the bird is directly across from you. Stop the action and explain the rules if children become confused.

Want to do more?

Once children become adept at managing two characters, add another "cat" to make the tag easier. A second cat will increase the frantic action to chase and escape. • Read *Frog, Duck, and Rabbit* by Susanna Gretz (Four Winds Press, 1992).

Involving parents

Parents and children can play a game of "Cat and Bird" at home. If there are fewer than six people, enlist the help of friends and neighbors and their children.

Cooperative Towers

4⁺

Our educational system is based on competition. Children are often pitted against each other in competing to be the first with the "right" answer. One child's failure to answer "correctly" becomes another's opportunity to succeed.

What to do

1. Invite the children to try a difficult cooperative game. Demonstrate by asking one child to be your partner. Begin by placing one block in the center of the table. Ask your partner to choose a block and place it on top of the one you just played.

2. If she succeeds, the turn passes back to you. You have to place a third block on the tower, either upon the first or second block.

3. Turns pass back and forth with each person attempting to balance an additional block on the tower.

4. Players can place blocks anywhere on the tower that they wish, as long as the first block played is the only block to touch the table. Once the tower collapses, the game is over. Count the number of blocks balanced and suggest trying to improve their score the next time.

Want to do more?

Limit the number of blocks to about twenty. Be sure to include several dowel rods of various widths and lengths to increase the challenge.
• You can increase the number of children in a group from two to four or five. • This activity can be made easier by increasing the size of the blocks and cutting them to a uni- form shape. The more slender the dowel rod, the more difficult the task. • Read *The Quarreling Book* by Charlotte Zolotow, illustrated by Garth Williams (Harper and Row, 1963).

Involving parents

Parents and children can play a game of "Cooperative Towers" using scrap blocks of wood or a combination of cans and food boxes stacked on the kitchen floor.

People words to use

cooperate
partner
balance

Center

Block area

Things you will need

- Several small wooden blocks, cut in various irregular sizes

Chair Jam

People words to use

cooperate
rules
together
equal

Center

Movement area

Things you will need

- One chair for every child
- Record turntable or tape player
- Music

Few things are more painful than being dropped out of a group for failing. Many of us can remember the embarrassment of losing in a spelling bee or leaving the group in a game of musical chairs. Failure becomes associated with rejection.

What to do

1. Tell the children they are going to play a game of musical chairs with different rules. Instead of dropping out of the game, everyone will stay. When the music stops, everyone must be seated either in a chair or in someone's lap. Instead of competing to sit one in each chair, the children will have to cooperate to sit together.

2. Set the chairs in back-to-back lines of equal length. Start the music. When it stops, take away one chair. The children will have to share a gradually diminishing number of chairs until everyone is piled up on one chair.

Want to do more?

Ask the children to form twosomes or threesomes to walk around the chairs. Ask these smaller groups to stay together throughout the game.

Involving parents

Parents can play a variation of this game using fewer chairs and singing a song instead of playing a record.

Telephone Friends

4⁺

Parents may unwittingly foster competition not only by comparing, but by reinforcing their children's achievements rather than the effort they make. For some parents, trying hard is not enough. Only success earns their love.

What to do

1. Punch a tiny hole in the center of one end of the cans with the screwdriver. Remove the other end. Cover any sharp edges with tape.

2. Ask the children to find a partner and visit the art area where they can work together, cooperate, to make telephones.

3. Set out the crayons and construction paper. Give each partnership two sheets of construction paper. Ask them to sit close together and work on a decoration for their telephones. When they are finished, help them glue their drawings to the cans.

4. Insert the ends of the string through the holes in the two cans. Make large knots so that neither end of the string can be removed.

5. Demonstrate how to stretch the string to talk and listen. Give them the phones and encourage them to have conversations in different places either inside or outside on the playground.

Want to do more?

Increase the length of the string to make the activity more challenging. • Or make two sets of telephones for each pair of children, so they can talk and listen at the same time. This requires much more coordination between them.

Involving parents

Partners can take turns bringing their telephones home to use with their parents.

People words to use

cooperate
friends
partner
together
conversation

Center

Art area

Things you will need

- One medium-sized empty tin can for each child
- Screwdriver
- Tape
- A 15′ length of string for every pair of children
- Construction paper cut to fit around the cans
- Glue
- Crayons

Crossing the Bridge

People words to use

cooperate
problem
help
group

Center

Movement area

Things you will need

• Two 8' lengths of 1" x 6" boards (Each board should be equal in length to a line of half your children standing side by side.)

Margaret Mead describes several noncompetitive cultures in her books. The Zunis and Iroquois both emphasize the basic principle of cooperative rather than individualistic behavior. Her research shows that competition is culturally conditioned, not an innate human characteristic.

What to do

1. Tell the children that you have a difficult problem for them to solve. Lay the boards flat, end to end, in a straight line. Ask half the group to line up on each board. Once everyone is on a board, say, "Let's pretend you are on a bridge. Let's see if everyone on one part of the bridge can get to the other side of the bridge. Help each other as much as you can. Do not step off the bridge until everyone has changed sides."

2. In the second round, lay the boards parallel to each other and about two feet apart. Challenge the children to cross from one bridge to the other.

Want to do more?

With older children, raise each bridge about three inches off the ground using building blocks. This increases the drama of the activity. • Increase the width of the boards to make the activity easier. • Read *Burgoo Stew* by Susan Patron, illustrated by Mike Shenon (Orchard, 1991).

Involving parents

Parents and children can play "Crossing the Bridge" at home, using boards or rolled rugs.

Hot Potato Stories

4+

In order to succeed with "Hot Potato Stories," children have to link their comments with those that precede them. They have to take turns and listen patiently until they have an opportunity to contribute.

What to do

1. Tell the children you have a cooperative game to play in which they will work together to make up their own special story. Tell them you will begin. After you tell the story for a short while, you will stop, and someone else will continue the story. Then another child will have a turn. After that child tells some of the story, someone else will keep it going, and so on until all the children have contributed to the story.

2. Once you are sure these instructions are understood, begin with the following "story stem" (or make up your own). Elaborate as you proceed, providing detail to make the story more interesting.

Once upon a time, a little girl and a little boy lived next door to each other and were friends. They were tired of being bossed around by all the adults. One day they decided to run away, so they gathered food into two little bags. When no one was watching, they left along a road near their homes.

Pretty soon the road went right into a forest. "This is strange," they thought, "We didn't know there was a forest near our homes." Well, they didn't want to go back, so on they went, right into that forest. At first, the air was warm, the sun sparkled down through the leaves, and they could hear beautiful bird sounds. But then the forest turned dark and cold, and scary sounds came from all around.

The children decided to leave the forest. When they turned to go back, though, the path was gone, replaced by big rocks and thorn bushes. With every step they took, the path disappeared behind them, for this was a magic path. Well, they had nowhere to go but straight ahead.

After a little bit, the path made a bend. They heard something coming from around that bend, something they could not see. But they could hear it coming. The two children stopped and hugged each other tightly. Then suddenly from around the bend came a....

At this point, invite children to keep the story going. No one should interrupt the new teller until she stops. You can repeat and ask simple questions to help the new speaker elaborate. ("Oh, no! It was a dragon! What color was it? Was it a nice or a mean dragon? What happened next?")

People words to use

cooperate
listen
patient
contribute
together
continue

Center

Circle time

Things you will need

- Nothing

3. When you think the children are ready to end the story, pick up the story line with a prepared ending. For example:

Suddenly, the little girl became very tired and lay down on the forest path. She immediately fell asleep. She awoke to someone shaking her arm. "No, no, get away," she thought. Then she opened her eyes. She was in her room, and her mother was shaking her arm. "Time to wake up and go to school, Sarah." "Oh, Mommy. I had the (funniest, scariest, most exciting) dream! It was about (briefly describe)."

"Wow, what a dream," her mother said. "That's for sure," replied Sarah. *The End.*

Want to do more?

Invite storytellers to your class to tell short stories to the children. Perhaps they can finish with a "Hot Potato Story" of their own. Use simpler stories and take less time when telling stories to younger children.

Involving parents

Children can teach their parents how to do "Hot Potato Stories" at home.

Cooperation, consideration of others, negotiation

Rope Runners

People words to use

cooperate
together
partner
obstacle

Center

Outside

Things you will need

- One 3' length of rope, knotted at both ends, for each pair of children

The simple act of movement is made much more complicated when linked with another person. "Rope Runners" requires constant awareness of and adjustment to another person. Partners must work together to be successful.

What to do

1. Ask the children to form partnerships and give each pair a rope. Ask each child to hold onto one end of the rope. Tell the children you would like to see how well they can cooperate with their partners.

2. Ask the partners to walk from one point to another without letting go of the rope. Then ask them to run together.

3. Set up a safe obstacle course for them to climb over and under, maintaining a grip on the rope at all times.

4. See whether they can stay together as they work toward other goals. Ask them, for example, to build a tower of large blocks or to

eat together during snack time or lunch.

5. Ask two partners to play simple games together like tag or catch.

Want to do more?

To increase the challenge, blindfold one of the children (supervise closely). • Play a game of cooperative musical chairs with partners (see "Chair Jam"). • Read *The Great Kapok Tree* by Lynne Cherry (Gulliver/ HBJ, 1990).

Involving parents

Parents and children can do "Rope Running" together at home.

Cooperative Drawing

4+

An activity like "Cooperative Drawing" can frustrate children who have not had prior experience with cooperation. To enjoy this activity, they must have learned the patience to cooperate. Children who find this one too difficult should be introduced to simpler cooperative activities like those in the beginning of this chapter.

What to do

1. Talk with the children for a few moments during circle time about cooperation. What is cooperation? Can they describe examples of co-operation? Tell them you have a cooperative activity for the art area. Ask the children to find a partner. Explain how many partners can work at the same time—one set for each ace bandage. Determine the order in which children will participate.

2. Ask the partners to sit close to each other at the table. Spread the paper between them and set out the crayons. Tell them that you would like to see if they can draw a picture with their arms tied together.

3. Wrap the ace bandage gently but firmly around the right wrist and lower arm of one child and the left wrist and lower arm of the other. Place crayons of different colors in their hands and ask them to begin.

4. Emphasize the rule that only the hands tied together can draw the picture.

5. If children are willing, you may repeat the process, switching hands.

Want to do more?

Partners can try finger painting instead of drawing. • Place a sponge between their wrists to increase comfort. • For additional challenge, blindfold one child, if he is willing, and place a crayon in his hand. The other partner is neither blindfolded nor given a crayon. After a drawing is made, switch sides. • Read *The Three Brothers* by Carolyn Croll (Putnam, 1991).

Involving parents

Parents and children can try "Cooperative Drawing" together, passing the drawing back and forth, unless more family members are involved.

People words to use

cooperate
partner
gentle
together

Center

Circle time
Art area

Things you will need

- Ace bandages, enough for each pair of children
- Crayons
- Large sheets of paper

Pick Up With Sticks

People words to use

cooperate
partner
volunteer
work together
group
encourage
opportunity

Center

Circle time

Things you will need

- Two slender lengths of wood, about 2' long and about 1" X 2"
- A balloon, nerf ball, tennis ball, golf ball or similar substitutes
- A container no higher than 1' to hold the balls (a large grocery bag, cut to about 6" in height would work)

Sometimes pairing children of a similar developmental level will be less frustrating for them than the results of random assignments or letting children choose their own partners.

What to do

1. Set the balloon and the container next to each other in the center of the circle. Tell the children you would like to see if they can cooperate with a partner to put the balloon into the bag. When one child volunteers to try, select a partner for him.

2. Give each child one of the wood sticks. Tell them the object of the game is for them to work together, to cooperate, to pick up the balloon with their sticks and place it into the bag. Encourage the rest of the group to cheer them on.

3. If they succeed with the balloon, continue with the nerf ball, then the tennis ball and, finally, the golf ball. If the balloon is too difficult, take turns being each child's partner, coaching them as you proceed. Step back and let them try as partners once again. Be generous with your words of encouragement as they work together.

4. When they are through, give others an opportunity to try as well.

Want to do more?

Vary the size, shape and firmness of the objects to be picked up. • Vary the lengths and shape of the sticks. Long dowel rods are the most difficult to handle. Make the task difficult enough to provide a challenge, but not so difficult as to be unnecessarily frustrating.

Involving parents

Parents and children can work together on a similar task at home. Suggest a simple activity like picking up a small crumpled piece of paper with two butter knives. For a more exciting challenge, try picking up a boiled egg.

Carry Board Teams

4⁺

Competitive societies tend to rush children toward adulthood. They are less likely to trust children to set their own pace toward success and work independently together outside of adult control.

What to do

1. Divide the children into pairs. Line up the partners at one end of the room. Set the rope down as a boundary at the other end of the room.

2. Give the first set of partners a board and ask them to hold the board parallel to the ground. Set a fairly stable object on the board. Tell the children you would like to see if they can cooperate to carry the object on their board across the boundary without letting it fall off.

3. While they are moving, comment on their ability to watch and adjust to their partner's actions. Encourage and praise their efforts.

4. When the first pair are about halfway across, repeat with the second pair in line.

Want to do more?

You can time the children as they move across the room and encourage them to move faster the next time they try. • Make the activity more difficult by creating obstacles the children have to move around and over. • Make it even more difficult by blindfolding one of the partners (supervise closely). • Read *The River Dragon* by Darcy Pattison, illustrated by Jean and Mou-sien Tseng (Lothrop, 1991).

Involving parents

Parents and children can do a similar activity at home using any long, narrow object in place of a board.

People words to use

cooperate
partner
boundary
encourage
work together

Center

Movement area

Things you will need

- Two 4′ lengths of a 1" x 5" board
- Objects that can be placed on the boards with various degrees of stability
- 6′ length of rope

Over the River

People words to use

cooperate
partner
cross
together
taking turns

Center

Movement area

Things you will need

- 15" strip of cloth
- Sponge
- One 8' length of a 1" x 6" board
- Two small area rugs

As children learn to share power voluntarily through cooperation, natural leadership talents begin to emerge. In a competitive society, adults prefer to remain in control. As a result, we have t-ball and Little Leagues instead of children just hanging out together and creating their own games.

What to do

1. Divide the children into pairs. Tell them you would like to see how well they cooperate.

2. Lay the board down, bridging the two rugs, and say, "Let's pretend this board is a bridge between two islands. The water is very deep. Let's see if you and your partner can cooperate to cross the bridge from one island to the other."

3. Ask the children to line up behind one of the islands. Tie the ankles of the first pair together, using a sponge to cushion their ankles if needed. Tell the children to work together to cross the bridge to the other island.

4. If they fall off, invite them to return to the end of the line to try again. If they fall off a second time, let them step back onto the board and continue.

5. Continue until all the children have had a turn.

Want to do more?

Change the difficulty level by increasing or decreasing the length of the board. • Try tying the children's hands together at the wrist. • Or invite three children to cross the bridge together. • Ask children to hold hands as they cross. If they break hands, they will have to begin over. • Read *King of the Playground* by Phyllis R. Naylor, illustrated by Nola Malone (Atheneum, 1991).

Involving parents

Parents and children can play "Over the River" at home, substituting a rolled rug for the boards, if necessary.

4⁺

Roller Ball

As in all cooperative games, the less direction the teacher gives, the more effective the activity. Demonstrate, encourage—and step away. Show children what to do, then cheer them on, giving further directions only if necessary. Step away from the leadership role if you can. Remain as a participant in the game.

People words to use

cooperate
teamwork
rules
difficulty
catcher
partner

Center

Block area

Things you will need

- A piece of thick poster-board approximately 36" x 24"
- A marble or very small ball
- Cup

What to do

1. Invite the children to find a partner and try a cooperative game. Demonstrate the game to explain the rules.

2. For this game, position the board at a sloping angle on top of a table so that the lower end of the board meets the very edge of the table. One child will position and roll the marble from the top of the slope to a partner holding a cup to catch it as it rolls off the end of the board.

3. Hand the marble to one child and the cup to the other, saying, "Start by rolling the marble from the top of the board. Let's see if your partner can catch it before it hits the floor."

4. Start with a gentle slope. Increase speed and difficulty by increasing the angle of the slope.

5. Encourage children to take turns rolling and catching.

Want to do more?

Increase the size of the ball and/or the cup to make the task easier.
• Try adding different textures to the slope's surface. Glue a few small pieces of wood to the surface to create barriers that affect the roll of the marble.

Involving parents

Parents can play a similar game at home with a piece of cardboard, a marble and a cup.

Class Garden

People words to use

cooperate
teamwork
seeds
growth
nurture
caretaker
environment
responsibilities

Center

Outside
Art area

Things you will need

- Seeds
- Garden tools
- Small green trees cut from green construction paper, one for each child
- Posterboard
- Marker

The "Class Garden" should be a shared, group effort. Instead of one child digging, planting, watering and weeding one plant, each child should have some responsibility for a large area if not the entire garden. For example, one child can water the garden, three can be responsible for removing weeds, etc.

What to do

1. Just before planting time arrives, have a circle time near the spot where your garden will be. Talk about seeds and growth. How does the earth nurture a seed so it grows? What do plants need to survive when they appear? Talk about what it means to be a caretaker or steward of the environment.

2. Discuss garden plans with the group. Where will the garden be? What kinds of plants will it contain? Use plants that mature early in the growing season. Show them the pictures on the seed packets. Make a list of all the tasks required on a posterboard. This will become the assignment board.

3. Go to the art area and help the children decorate and write their names on the small green tree shapes.

4. Ask the children to bring their trees back to circle time. Set up the posterboard. Go over the responsibilities involved in beginning the garden. Engage the children in deciding what they will do. Tape each child's tree next to her assignment on the board.

5. Change responsibilities and make adjustments on the assignment board as your garden progresses.

Want to do more?

When the garden begins to mature, take Polaroid pictures to give the children.

Involving parents

Encourage parents to start a small family garden or indoor potted plant arrangement. Family members can share responsibilities for the plants.

Not Enough

In this activity, something is offered to the group which cannot easily be divided among its members. The situation produces a conflict that the group then seeks to resolve. Enterprising four year olds in one of my groups solved the problem of being given four balloons by: suggesting that I go to the store to buy more (they all thought that was a good idea, but did not want to wait); that I not give them away at all (most disagreed with this idea); that I cut them in half (a few pointed out that this would not work); and, finally, that I give away four now and bring more to give away the next day. The group decided that this last suggestion was the best. Through a gradual process of negotiation, the children selected four in their group to receive the four balloons.

What to do

1. Tell the children that you have something to give them, but before you can proceed there is a problem they must solve. Set out the objects and say something like, "I would like to give you these, but I think we may have a problem. What do you think it is?" After the children identify the problem—not enough to go around—ask for their help finding a solution.

2. Engage the children in discussing how the objects should be given out. Do not impose your solution. Try to have the children discover some mutually agreeable solution of their own. See that everyone's ideas are discussed. Encourage the children to make their own decisions. Point out the consequences of suggested choices. For example, ask, "What would happen if we cut them in half?"

3. If the group cannot find an acceptable solution, you may suggest alternatives for them to discuss.

Want to do more?

Decrease the size of the group to make the problem solving easier.
• Read *The Doorbell Rang* by Pat Hutchins (Morrow, 1989).

Involving parents

Parents can also introduce simple conflicts for their children to negotiate. "There is only one piece of pie left. What shall we do?" Or "You both want to play with this truck. How can we solve this problem?"

People words to use

cooperate
problem solving
negotiation
solution
alternatives
agree
choices

Center

Circle time

Things you will need

• About three or four objects the children will want to have

Won or Two

People words to use

problem solving
partner
generous
consideration

Center

Circle time

Things you will need

- A napkin for pair of children
- One nutritious cookie (or other food) for each child

Children may respond to this activity in several ways: the recipient may promptly consume the cookie; the cookie may be accepted and divided and a portion returned to the original giver; the cookie may be given only after considerable negotiation. Many possibilities exist when the second cookie is then placed on the napkin. Children who divide the first cookie are likely to repeat that "equity" strategy. Most of the children who give without receiving in the first round are likely to wait to receive the second cookie from their partner. In some cases, children will give both cookies to their partners without hesitation.

What to do

1. Ask the children to wash their hands thoroughly. When they are ready for circle time, tell them you have cookies to give them. Tell them that, however, they will have to find a partner and solve a problem first. Once everyone has a partner, ask them to sit facing each other around the circle.

2. Place the napkins between the pairs of children. Put one cookie on one partner's napkin. Ask the children not to touch the cookie yet. Explain, "Here is the problem. The rule is that you can only get the cookie if your partner gives it to you. You cannot take it for yourself." Remind the children of this guideline if they forget.

3. Ask them to begin. Remind them that they cannot take the cookie for themselves. When all the cookies have been given away, put out a second cookie for each pair.

4. Ask the children how they solved the problem. Emphasize the cooperation that took place.

5. If someone has been left without a cookie, consider giving one to them and thanking them for their generosity

Want to do more?

Use small inexpensive trinkets and other giveaways instead of cookies.
• Begin with two different food items placed on the napkin. • Read *Full Moon Soup* by Alastaire Graham (Dial, 1991).

Involving parents

Emphasize to parents the importance of getting children to think about conflict rather than simply following through with adult suggestions. They can encourage children to become confident problem solvers. Engage them in brainstorming many possible solutions to a conflict. Once this pool of ideas is created, then begin choosing a solution.

4+

Jet Plane

You will need at least seven children for this activity. Supervise them closely. Be one of the lifters only if you have to do so for safety's sake. You may have trouble cooperating with the children on this task because of the size difference. Also, if you become too involved, children may look to you for guidance rather than working together as a group.

What to do

1. Involve the children in a brief discussion about airplanes and flying. After a few moments, ask if one of them would like to pretend to be a jet. Other children in the group will cooperate to help the jet fly.

2. Ask the volunteer to lie down on her stomach and spread her arms straight out to the side to form wings. Ask the other children to get on their hands and knees and crowd around both sides of the volunteer. When they are in position, ask them to slide their arms under her chest and legs.

3. When everyone is ready, ask the lifters to stand slowly at the same time and raise the jet off the ground. Once everyone is standing, ask the lifters to fly the jet slowly across the room. After a brief flight, ask them to land the jet slowly.

4. While the jet is flying, tell the lifters something like, "You are doing a great job cooperating together. Great!"

5. Repeat with other volunteers.

Want to do more?

If your group is big enough, you can have two jets flying at the same time. A small area rug can serve as a landing strip. The jets can take off and land on the "runway."

Involving parents

Explain the activity so that parents and older children and other friends or relatives can take younger ones for a flight.

People words to use

cooperate
help
gentle
volunteer

Center

Movement area

Things you will need

- Nothing

Rocket Ship

People words to use

cooperate
help
trust
volunteer

Center

Movement area

Things you will need

- A small, sturdy, child-sized chair

Cooperative games depend on trust. Everyone is expected to contribute to the extent of their ability. Individuals in the group rely on each other to do their share.

What to do

1. Set the chair in the center of the circle. Talk with children for a few moments about rocket ships. "Has anyone flown in a plane?"

2. Tell the children you would like to pretend the chair is actually a rocket ship. Ask if someone would like to take a ride in the rocket ship. Have the volunteer sit in the chair.

3. The remaining children crowd around the chair, finding the best available handhold. Count down from ten. On "blast-off," everyone slowly lifts the chair. Supervise carefully and help when needed. With the rocket ship elevated, go for a short cruise around the room. Return to the launch pad.

4. Repeat with other volunteers.

Want to do more?

Use a small area rug to provide rides on a "magic carpet." • Read *Time Train* by Paul Fleischman, illustrated by Claire Ewart (Harper Collins, 1991).

Involving parents

Parents can take their children for rocket rides at home on a sturdy chair. Adult friends or older children should try only if a parent is available.

Rubber Band

5+

Research shows that, over time, children gradually begin to prefer easy tasks to challenging ones. Fear of failure erodes the adventuresome spirit prevalent in young children.

What to do

1. Tie the ends of the rope together.

2. Place the rope on the floor in a circle. Ask all the children to grab the rope and pick it up together. Ask them to face the center of the circle and take one step after another, backwards, until the rope is stretched as far as it will go.

3. Tell the children you would like to see how well they can cooperate. You would like them to move in the same direction, keeping the rope stretched as much as possible. Ask the group to move toward a nearby object.

4. Remind them that everyone has to work together to keep the rope stretched.

5. If the group moves successfully, ask them to cover more distance. Ask them to walk faster and then slower.

Want to do more?

For an added challenge, call the game "Rubber Band Leader." Ask one child to go to the center. The rest of the group has to keep the circle stretched around her as she walks. Can they keep the leader in the center? • When you yell "Switch!" everyone drops the rope, runs to the center, then returns to a new spot in the circle. • To add to the challenge, ask everyone to go inside the circle, raise the rope behind them and take steps backward until the rope is totally stretched. Ask them to let go of the rope with their hands. See if they can maintain the tension in the rope so that it will remain off the ground as they move as a group from one point to another.

Involving parents

Parents and children can try "Rubber Band" at home, involving friends and relatives if needed to make a large enough group.

People words to use

cooperate
teamwork
group

Center

Movement area

Things you will need

- A rope equivalent in length to a line of all your children standing side by side

Mule Team

People words to use

cooperate
teamwork
help
problem solving
volunteer

Center

Circle time
Movement area

Things you will need

- 6' length of rope

Like many games in this book, "Mule Team" should emphasize cooperative effort rather than successfully crossing the boundary. The boundary is there as a goal for the group. What counts is that they work together. Emphasize effort, not achievement.

What to do

1. Begin with the following story:

   Once upon a time there was a miner who worked in a gold mine. He worked and worked and worked until he found lots of gold. He was so excited because he had finally found the treasure he had hoped was there. He gathered it all up in a bag and got ready to go to the bank in town. But the gold was too heavy for him to carry. Oh, no! Now what was he to do? He couldn't carry it by himself. One of his friends stopped by and gave him a mule. But the bag was still too heavy. Then another friend stopped by and gave him another mule. But still the bag was too heavy. Then another friend brought a third mule. Now he had enough help. If they cooperated, all worked together, the miner and the mules could carry the gold to the bank. *The End.*

2. Invite the children to pretend to solve the miner's problem. Ask for three volunteers to pretend to be mules, one to be the miner and another to be the sack of gold.

3. Lay the rope down at one end of the room. If the children cross the rope, they have reached the bank.

4. Bring the volunteers to the opposite side of the room. Have the three "mules" get on their hands and knees, close together and facing the same direction. Help the "bag of gold" lie on his stomach across the backs of the mules. The miner should remain near the mules, helping to keep the gold on their backs. When everybody is ready, cheer them on to reach the bank.

Want to do more?

Set up an obstacle course of pillows or rolled blankets or rugs for the mule team to cross on the way to the goal. Supervise closely.

Involving parents

Two adults or older children can work together to provide a "Mule Team" ride for younger children.

Copy Cat

5⁺

The activities in this and other chapters build on one another. Five year olds who have little experience with this type of activity may find one like "Copy Cat" frustrating. If they do, regardless of their age, start with the simpler activities found earlier in each chapter and work your way to the more difficult.

What to do

1. Set chair number one down in the center of the circle. Set chair number two directly behind chair number one, facing the same direction. Place chair number three so it faces chair number one. Shift chair number two slightly to the side so it has a clear view of chair number three.

2. Tell the children you have a "copy cat" game for them to try. Ask for three volunteers to sit in the chairs. Give instructions when the children are ready.

3. Whisper in the ear of the child sitting in chair number two to hold one hand up in the air. Ask number three to act like a mirror and copy whatever number two does. Ask number one to act like a mirror and copy whatever number three does. At this point, number one and number two should be making the identical gesture. Go to the next step if they have understood so far.

4. Invite the child in chair number two to perform very slow movements with her arms and hands. See if all three can work together to create a similar motion.

5. After a few minutes, let the threesome change positions. When each has had a turn, let another group of three try.

Want to do more?

Instead of making arm or hand gestures, number two can try facial expressions. • For greater challenge, remove the chairs and ask number two to make any type of slow motion movement in place.

Involving parents

Encourage parents to play a simple mirror game with their children. One person slowly makes a face or a motion while the other copies. Roles can be reversed to provide opportunities to be both a leader and a follower.

People words to use

cooperate
identical
volunteer

Center

Movement area

Things you will need

- Three chairs

Card Partners

People words to use

cooperate
problem solving
guess
describe
choice

Center

Art area

Things you will need

- Several four-card sets, two cards with identical faces and two with different ones (see the illustration).
- A barrier between partners that will allow them to see each other's faces but not their hands (e.g. a felt board sandwiched between blocks).

Making the pictures fairly similar will challenge children to find the right words to help their partners choose correctly.

What to do

1. Set the barrier up on a table.

2. Ask the children to find a partner with whom to play this game. They will have to work together to solve a problem. One child will be a "teller" and the other a "guesser."

3. Have the partners sit on opposite sides of the barrier. Give the "teller" one picture and the "guesser" a complete set of cards.

4. Ask the teller to describe his card to the guesser. The guesser then chooses one card from his set, shows it to the teller and asks, "Is this it?"

5. If the guesser is incorrect, ask the teller to describe the picture a little more. Give the teller hints for making a more thorough description. If the guesser's choice is correct, ask the partners to switch roles and continue with another set of cards.

Want to do more?

Make the activity more challenging by using more abstract drawings and increasing the number of different cards given to the guesser.

Involving parents

Make several sets of cards and directions for children to take home. The children can teach their parents how to play at home.

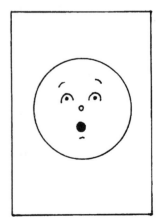

Partner Kickball

5+

As children move through school, their self-confidence is gradually eroded as their achievements become more exclusively associated with winning. There is only room for one person at the top.

What to do

1. Ask the children to find a partner. Tell them you would like to see how well they cooperate to kick a ball into a goal. They will have to work together because one leg will be tied to their partner's.

2. Set the box on its side at one end of the room. Ask the partners to line up at the opposite end. Place the right leg of one partner and the left leg of the other close together and tie securely, but not too tightly, at the ankle with the strip of cloth and the sponge between their ankles as a cushion.

3. Set the ball in front of the two children and tell them the object of the game is to kick the ball with their tied legs into the box on the other side of the room before the timer goes off.

4. Set the timer for about three minutes and ask the children to begin.

5. When the timer goes off or they reach the goal, repeat with the second pair in the line.

Want to do more?

To change the level of difficulty, increase or decrease the size of the box and/or the ball. • Try having two pairs of children kick two balls into the same box. When one pair is successful, they can go help the other. • For a real challenge, tell the children to kick the ball backwards.

Involving parents

Parents and children can play "Partner Kickball" at home.

People words to use

cooperate
goal
partner
teamwork

Center

Movement area

Things you will need

- Medium-sized box
- Large, soft ball
- 15" strip of cloth
- Timer
- Sponge

Drop in the Bucket

People words to use

cooperate
guide
partner
exchange
direct

Center

Movement area

Things you will need

- Small soft ball
- Large grocery bag or cardboard box
- Blindfold

Comparison is a natural part of growing up and evaluating one's abilities. Such evaluation need not be competitive. Each person should be able to reach a goal and help others along the way. One person's success need not depend on another person's failure. The success of one can inspire the other to succeed.

What to do

1. In this activity, the blindfolded child is guided by a partner to drop a ball into a container.

2. *Round 1*: The blindfolded partner takes the ball and turns several times in place. He then holds the ball out for the other partner to catch in the container.

3. *Round 2*: Set the container next to or behind the blindfolded child. Invite his partner to direct him to drop the ball into the container. Let them exchange roles and repeat as desired. If they are proficient at this activity, they may move to round 3.

4. *Round 3*: After one partner is blindfolded, place the container several feet away and put the ball into the container. Now the goal is for the child to direct his blindfolded partner to the container to remove the ball. Repeat as desired. Once round 3 is completed, invite them to try round 4.

5. *Round 4*: After one partner is blindfolded, give him the ball and place the container several feet away. The partner then guides the blindfolded child across the room to drop the ball into the container.

6. Remain close to the blindfolded child to ensure safety.

Want to do more?

With older children, you can place stationary obstacles like chairs or even other children in the mover's path to increase the difficulty. Supervision becomes even more important when such obstacles are used. As in "Night Flying" in the "Kindness" chapter, you may have to help the partners understand simple directions for movement.
- Read *No Need For Monty* by James Stevenson (Greenwillow, 1987).

Involving parents

Parents and children can play "Drop in the Bucket" at home.

Peace Table

The "Peace Table" creates a setting that provides a retreat from conflict so that discussion and problem solving can take place. The presence of the Peace Table is a clear signal to stop hitting, yelling or crying and start talking.

What to do

1. Ask the children for examples of disagreements. Describe a few of your own. How do people feel when they disagree? What can happen when there is an argument?

2. Spread the felt blanket out in the center of your circle. Tell the children that this blanket is the group's Peace Table. When there is a disagreement, those involved can have a "sit down" around the Peace Table to talk and find a way to solve the problem.

3. Teach the group the following poem:

   Come to the Peace Table,
   A place to be free.
   What you want, and I want,
   We can talk to agree.

4. Take a small toy and lay it in the center of the blanket. Say something like, "Let's pretend _____ (name a child) and _____ (name a child) both want to play with this _____ toy. They will sit on opposite sides of the table. I will sit on another side of the table to help them talk to solve their problem. Neither one can take the toy until a solution is found. Does anyone have any ideas how a disagreement about who gets to play with the toy could be solved?" Ask the children for their ideas.

5. After a few moments of discussion, go to the art area to decorate the Peace Table. Write each child's name somewhere on the Peace Table.

6. In the future, when there is a disagreement, bring out the Peace Table as a way to prompt discussion and problem solving. Use the felt blanket **only** for thisukj nbbbbbbbbb purpose.

Want to do more?

Once the children become accustomed to solving problems with the Peace Table, you may find them using it without your help. Your assistance as a mediator will be valuable, but independent problem solving, without your help, is the ideal. • The Peace Table will calm children down and help to focus conversation on seeking agreement. It is a symbol of nonviolence. • Read *Tiger Watch* by Jan Wahl, illustrated by Charles Mikolaycak (Harcourt Brace Jovanovich, 1982).

Involving parents

Parents and children can make their own Peace Table at home to use when disagreements arise.

People words to use

peace
agreement
problem solving
discussion

Center

Circle time
Art area

Things you will need

- Large piece of felt, at least 3' x 5'
- Decorative materials (bits of felt and cloth, glimmer, tiny stars, etc.)
- Markers
- White glue

Chapter Four

Kindness

Dear Parents,

Our focus on friendship, compassion and cooperation has provided a foudations for the development of kindness, the fourth and last major goal of The Peaceful Classroom Program. The ability to offer, accept and ask for kindness is a critical part of social relationships. The person who cannot be kind is isolated, if not rejected by others throughout life.

The Peaceful Classroom Program views kindness as a combination of several complementary skills: caretaking, gentleness, helping, generosity, sharing, protection and encouragement. We hope to nurture each of these skills in children.

Young children are naturally "egocentric." This does not mean that they are selfish. Young children's kindness is always offered from their own point of view instead of understanding the other person's needs. A toddler, for example, may try to comfort his sick mother while she sleeps by giving her his teddy bear. The teddy bear comforts him so he believes that it will do the same for his mother. As children grow older, they are better able to offer more effective help from the perspective of the person who needs it.

We will use words like "care," "gentle," "generous" and "protect" in our discussions with children. Children will participate in group activities like "The Ouchie," "Lotion Motion" and "Poor Little Sad Eyes." We will also be reading carefully selected picture books that focus on kindness. Each component of The Peaceful Classroom Program will be sensitive to the ages of the children involved. We will stay in touch with you about the program as it proceeds. We are also interested in hearing any questions or suggestions you might have.

Sincerely,

Growing Flowers

3⁺

Understanding the needs of living things is a prerequisite for caretaking. Gentleness is based on respect and appreciation. A simple activity involving the care of a plant is a good way to begin.

What to do

1. Show the plant to children. Talk about what the plant needs to grow. Emphasize the importance of being gentle when touching the flower. What would happen if someone grabbed or slapped it? Invite the children to touch and smell the flower gently, one at a time.

2. Talk to the children about how a flower grows from a tiny seed. Begin with the planting of the seed, then describe watering, sprouting and stem and leaf growth.

3. Act out the following fingerplay with the children:

   Tiny seed planted just right.
   Not a breath of air, nor a ray of light.
   (Cover right fist with left hand)
   Rain falls slowly to and fro,
   And now the seed begins to grow.
   (Remove left hand and slowly uncurl right fist)
   Slowly reaching for the light
   With all its energy, all its might.
   (Right hand makes creeping motion upwards with fingers together)
   The little seed's work is almost done,
   To grow up tall and face the sun.
   (Stretch out fingers of right hand)

Want to do more?

With older children, pass the plant around the circle. Emphasize being gentle. • Ask the children to bring a potted plant from home to show the group. • Compare two plants with different needs for sun and water, for example, a cactus and a philodendron.

Involving parents

Encourage parents to give their children the responsibility of caring for a potted plant at home. They should make sure their children understand what to do to care properly for the plant.

People words to use

life
growing up
care
gentle
respect
appreciation

Center

Circle time

Things you will need

• Flowering potted plant

Plant Life

People words to use

life
grow
gentle
care
germinate

Center

Circle time
Science area

Things you will need

- Enough seeds for all the children (use dill, chive, marigold or other seeds that germinate quickly)
- A container filled with dirt for each child
- Marker

In this activity children are given the responsibility of planting a seed and caring for the plant that sprouts over a period of time. They will need to be reminded every day of their responsibility to care for the growing plant. Consider posting a list of duties with all their names that they can check off after completing tasks.

What to do

1. Take the seeds out of the package and show them to the children. Talk about seeds and discuss how they grow when put into dirt and watered.

2. Place the containers on the table. Ask the children to plant their seeds. Label the containers with the children's names and place them in a sunny spot.

3. Water and care for the plants. A check-off chart listing necessary care and the children's names is helpful.

4. Talk with the children about the care that seeds need to help them grow. Extend the discussion to the care babies and young children need to grow to healthy adulthood.

Want to do more?

Let children take the plants home after they begin to germinate and grow. • Ask the children to keep their plants with them for a period of time. If they take them outside, for example, they should find a safe place for the plants while they play. • Depending on the season, children can replant their plant outside in a small school garden. Responsibility for watering and weeding can be divided among the children.

Involving parents

Encourage parents and children to grow their own windowsill herb garden of chives.

3⁺

Adopt a Tree

This activity asks children to become involved with life outside their classroom, life over which they have little control. They begin here to expand the radius of their responsibility.

What to do

1. Tell the children that they are going to find a little tree outside for the class to "adopt." This means that everyone will have some responsibility for keeping the tree healthy so that it will grow up big and strong.

2. Take the children outside and look for the youngest tree within easy walking distance of your school.

3. Sit around the tree and discuss what it needs to be healthy. What kind of care does the tree need from the children? How will this care change over the rest of the school year? Identify the specific caretaking actions the children will do: pulling weeds, trimming grass, fertilizing, providing water from buckets, mulching around the base of the trunk and checking for harmful bugs.

4. During the next week, assign responsibilities for taking care of the tree and form a plan for continued care for the rest of the year.

5. Revisit the tree occasionally to check its progress.

Want to do more?

Invite a horticulturist to visit your group to talk about caring for trees. • Conduct a field trip to a lawn and garden store. • Read *A Mother for Choco* by Keiko Kasza (Putnam, 1992).

Involving parents

Parents and children can visit a local park and adopt a young tree growing in a primitive area that receives no maintenance from park personnel. They can take care of the tree during periodic visits. A picnic near the tree may be nice at certain times of the year.

People words to use

life
growing up
gentle
care
responsibility
healthy

Center

Outside

Things you will need

- Fertilizer
- Water buckets
- Simple gardening tools

3+

Gentle People

People words to use

gentle
careful
kind

Center

Circle time

Things you will need

- A small, tame pet like a guinea pig or hamster

Pets provide wonderful opportunities for children to learn gentleness and care-taking. Since a pet's sudden movements may startle a child or lead to rough handling, stay with the pet when you let a child hold it. Be particularly cautious with children who have a history of aggression. Even the most active child can be very gentle when it comes to handling animals. Be aware that deliberately rough treatment of an animal is usually preceded by silly behavior.

What to do

1. Ask the children if they understand what gentleness means. Discuss various ways people can be gentle with each other. Tell the group that you would like to give them the opportunity to be gentle.

2. Bring the pet into the circle and explain that you would like to see how gentle they can be. Giving assistance where needed, pass the animal around the circle. Bypass children who do not want to handle the animal and gently take it away from those who are too rough. Clearly identify any inappropriate behavior and suggest more suitable responses. Comment on any gentle behavior you see, saying something like, "Gee, Carl, you sure are gentle with the guinea pig. You are being very careful and kind."

Want to do more?

The same activity can be done with an egg if you hesitate to use an animal. • Read *Rockabye Farm* by Diane Johnston Hamm, illustrated by Rick Brown (Simon and Schuster, 1992).

Involving parents

Parents can take their children to a neighbor's or relative's house to meet and hold a pet. Or they can visit the pet store to hold various animals.

3+

I Cannot See

This activity introduces blindfolds to children. Children will have the opportunity to see how a blindfold works without having to wear one themselves. They will also have a simple opportunity to help another person. You should have an assistant in the room with you to supervise the children while you wear the blindfold.

What to do

1. Talk with the children about "blindness." Have they ever met someone who is blind? How do blind people learn about the world around them? Discuss why other senses like touch, sound and smell are important for blind people. Show the objects you selected and discuss how a blind person could experience each one.

2. Tell the children that you would like to pretend to be a blind person. During the time you are wearing the blindfold, you would like them to find things in the classroom to bring to you to touch, smell or hear.

3. Put on the blindfold and ask the children to make their selections. As the children bring objects to you, take a few moments to touch, smell and listen to them by shaking or tapping them. When you are through, give them back to the children to return to their original place.

4. After exploring each object, remove the blindfold and gather the children around you to thank them for their help. Summarize what you experienced.

Want to do more?

For an added challenge, ask one child to take you to a specific location in the classroom. • You can introduce this activity on three consecutive days, asking first only for things to smell, then things to hear and, finally, to touch. • Try the activity outside if you have other adults to supervise the children. • Read *Berlioz the Bear* by Jan Brett (Putnam, 1991).

Involving parents

Parents can close their eyes at home or outside, and children can bring them things to touch, smell and hear.

People words to use

blind
touch
sound
smell
kindness
help

Center

Circle time

Things you will need

- One blindfold
- Three objects that make a sound or can be touched or smelled

Nature Tribute

People words to use

gentle
nature
gifts
celebrate
kindness

Center

Circle time
Outside

Things you will need

- Natural things in your area

Learning to respect nature begins during the preschool years. Preschoolers are animistic in their thinking—they view all the life around them as having consciousness and motivation. They are readily inclined to respond to a tree or bush as though it has feelings.

What to do

1. Discuss the idea that people can be kind to nature as well as to people. Give examples of such kindness: keeping a picnic area clean, leaving wildflowers unpicked so others can appreciate them, or providing fertilizer and water to a tree or plant. Tell the children you have an activity that lets them be kind to nature.

2. Pay tribute to a nearby object of nature, such as a tree, large rock or plant. (See also "Adopt a Tree.") Each group member looks for an interesting object found in nature—leaves, twigs, pebbles, moss or feathers—to decorate the object. Ask the children to sit around or close to the object and encourage them to discuss what they like about it. Invite them to touch the object gently and place their decoration on or near it. Ask them to chant the following poem with you:

   Hello little _____, (tree, plant, rock, bush)
   You are so dear.
   Thank you for living
   And just being here.

3. You can also sing a song or play a game around the object.

Want to do more?

Search the area around the object for litter. What belongs and what does not belong in nature? Collect and remove the trash.• With four year olds and older, read *Brother Eagle, Sister Sky: A Message from Chief Seattle* illustrated by Susan Jeffers, (Dial, 1991).

Involving parents

Teach the poem to parents. The family can gather around something near their home.

Bird Dinner

3+

In their efforts to care for wildlife, children have less control than they do with plant life. Animals are capable of caring for themselves but benefit from the kindness of others. Choose a time of year when food for birds is scarce.

What to do

1. During circle time discuss the care and feeding of wildlife. If food for birds is scarce in winter in your area, discuss why this is so. Talk about various ways we can be kind to wildlife.

2. Invite the children to visit the science area during free play to make special bird dinners.

3. Have the children roll pine cones or apples in shortening or peanut butter, then dip them into bird seed.

4. Tie with string, leaving loose ends for hanging the bird meals.

5. The children can also gently roll a string of dry cereal in peanut butter and attach additional string for hanging.

6. Place the bird meals in the box as they are completed.

7. When the children have finished making the meals, gather in a circle to talk about their concern and kindness. Take them outside and ask them to choose a nearby tree from which to hang or drape their meals. If possible, select a tree that can be seen from your school.

8. After hanging the meals on the tree, invite the children to join hands in a circle around the tree and repeat the following poem with you:

Hey little birds—
Here's something new
To help you live—
A meal for you.

Want to do more?

Depending on where you live, choose an appropriate meal for a different type of wildlife. • Read *Ben and the Porcupine* by Carol Carrick, illustrated by Donald Carrick (Houghton Mifflin, 1981).

Involving parents

Parents can also make bird dinners at home to drape on trees in their backyards.

People words to use

kind
care
hunger
wildlife

Center

Circle time
Science area
Outside

Things you will need

- Pine cones or apples
- Shortening or peanut butter
- Round oat cereal
- Birdseed
- String
- Scissors
- Box

Growing Up

People words to use

baby
growing up
healthy
care
gentle

Center

Circle time
Art area

Things you will need

- A four to ten month old baby accompanied by a parent (if a real infant is not available, substitute a doll)
- An infant toy like a stuffed animal, rattle, ball
- Infant clothing
- Several infant care products

Children will be challenged to be especially careful in the way they respond to and handle a baby. They will have to hold the child firmly without squeezing too hard and support its body properly, especially the head. This special care will encourage children to adjust to another person's needs.

What to do

1. Introduce the parent and baby to the children. Ask the parent to talk about the baby things he brought to show. If possible, allow the children to come up and touch the baby. Some children may even be allowed to hold the baby in their laps for a few moments.

2. Ask the children the following questions:

   What are some things you can do that this baby cannot do?

   How are you different from this baby?

   Summarize and restate their comments as you go along. Emphasize the idea that children are changing as they grow up. As they grow, their abilities increase.

3. Discuss the type of care an infant needs to grow up healthy. What do mothers and fathers do to care for their babies?

4. Thank the visitors for coming to your class. With the parent's permission, invite the children to give the baby a gentle pat or hug as a friendly goodbye.

5. As a follow-up, ask the children to draw a picture of the baby. Collect the pictures and send them to the parent who made the visit.

Want to do more?

Children can bring their baby pictures to show to the group. • Read *Do You Know What I'll Do?* by Charlotte Zolotow, illustrated by Garth Williams (Harper and Row, 1958).

Involving parents

Parents can show preschoolers their infant toys or clothes if these were saved. Parents can also tell the child how he reacted to their care—their feeding him or giving him a bath, for example.

3+

The Ouchie

The goal of this activity is to encourage children to offer care to others, not to apply Band-Aids correctly. Young children may need help putting Band-Aids on their partner, but keep in mind that this is not a technical lesson in first aid.

What to do

1. Ask the children if they have ever cut themselves. What is blood? Have they ever seen anyone bleed? What does "hurt" mean? Tell the children you have an activity in which they can help each other with a pretend "ouchie" (or, as they say in some parts of the country, "boo-boo").

2. Take out the paint and brush and tell them that you have a pretend cut. Take a little red paint and dab it on your finger. Say, "Oh, I have a pretend cut on my finger. Can someone help me?" Ask the volunteer helper to use the sponge and paper towel to clean and dry your "ouchie." Then ask the helper to put a Band-Aid on your finger.

3. Ask the children to find a partner. Tell them that they will help each other with pretend ouchies. Give a sponge, paper towel and Band-Aid to each pair. Go around the circle, asking the partners which one is pretending to be hurt and which one is the helper. Hurt children indicate where they want the ouchie to be. Dab a small amount of paint on this spot. The helper then uses the sponge, paper towel and Band-Aid to clean and protect the "wound."

4. Allow the children to switch roles and repeat the process once more.

Want to do more?

Ask an emergency medical technician to visit your class and give a few simple first aid lessons. • Read *Aki and the Fox* by Akiko Hayashi (Doubleday, 1991).

Involving parents

The next time a parent has a simple cut, he can involve his child in administering first aid. Even though parents may perform first aid faster and better, asking children to help strengthens their self-esteem and gives them practice in caretaking.

People words to use

hurt
helping
blood
care
fear
sadness

Center

Circle time

Things you will need

- Thick red paint and a small brush
- Small, wet sponges and dry paper towels (one for each child and teacher)
- Band-Aids (one for each child and a few extras)

Know See

People words to use

help
blind
senses
sight
touch
smell
hear
give
pretend

Center

Circle time

Things you will need

- Two blindfolds

By blindfolding yourself, you challenge children to relate to you with words and touch rather than visual cues. "Teacher, look at this!" will no longer work. Be sure an aide or another teacher will supervise your children before attempting this activity. If you are not comfortable making a commitment to keep the blindfold on, do not introduce this activity. Avoid giving in to the temptation to peek. Challenge yourself to experience this sensory deprivation.

What to do

1. Tell the children you would like to find out what it would be like to be a pretend "blind" person in their class. Discuss and clarify any misconceptions they have about blindness. Emphasize that you plan to wear the blindfold for the morning but can remove it if necessary. Tell them that you will need their help while you wear the blindfold. Invite them to try wearing one for a short while, too.

2. Put on the blindfold and describe what you hear, smell, feel around you.

3. Keep the blindfold on as long as you can. Share your thoughts and feelings with the children while wearing the blindfold. Ask for their help when needed.

4. When you are ready to remove the blindfold, gather the children in a circle and share your experiences.

Want to do more?

If you do this activity with older children, let a volunteer take you for a walk outside in a protected area. • Read *Nathan's Balloon Adventure* by Lulu Delacre (Scholastic Hardcover, 1991).

Involving parents

Parents can let their children take them for a blind walk around the inside of their home.

Lotion Motion

4⁺

This activity provides children with a fun way to make gentle contact with each other. A good time for this activity is immediately after hand washing following their lunch or snack.

What to do

1. Ask the children to find a partner and sit facing each other. Go around the room and put lotion in each child's hand. Ask the children to find out how the lotion feels by rubbing their hands together. After a few moments, ask them to join hands with their partner. Encourage them to explore each other's hands in a massaging motion.

2. Call the group together and have everyone make a close, friendly circle. All the children can reach their hands into the middle of the circle and touch each other's hands. Pour extra lotion over their hands and encourage everyone to explore the different textures. Emphasize gentle contact. Encourage motion by suggesting that the hands on the bottom move to the top in a repeated cycle.

Want to do more?

Instead of lotion, place one small lump of soft playdough in each child's hands. Can they knead the dough together?

Involving parents

Describe this activity for parents to try with their children at home. "Lotion Motion" can be fun with feet, too.

People words to use

gentle
partner
join

Center

Circle time

Things you will need

- Hand lotion

4+

Are You Sick?

People words to use

sick
gentle
yucky feelings
care

Center

Circle time

Things you will need

- Blanket
- Pillow
- Washcloth
- Bowl with a **small** amount of warm water

A relatively complex act like caretaking can be broken down into its fundamental components. Cooling a person's forehead with a washcloth or covering another with a blanket are simple caretaking skills young children can learn and practice. By fourteen months, children will pat and stroke someone in distress. Beyond eighteen months, their caretaking becomes more sophisticated, including hugging, seeking adult help and finding comforting objects such as blankets and toys. In this activity, provide simple, easily understood explanations of the causes and consequences of being sick or hurt. Avoid using the word "bug" to refer to bacteria or viruses. Describe and discuss symptoms of illness like sore throat, cough, fever, upset stomach. Provide factual reassurance to children who are frightened about an illness or accident.

What to do

1. Ask the children if they have ever been sick. Take a few moments to discuss times when they were ill.

2. Introduce the activity with the following story:

   Once upon a time in Butterberry Hill, Amy became very sick. Her mommy brought her a blanket and pillow so she could lay down. Because Amy was sick, her temperature went up, and she became very hot. Her mommy and daddy took a damp washcloth and gently washed her face to make her feel cooler. After two days of rest and loving care, Amy felt better and could go to school once again. *The End*.

3. Tell the children that you have an activity in which they will pretend to care for someone who is sick. Ask for a volunteer to pretend to be sick. Ask the volunteer to go to the center of the circle and lie down on his back. Ask him to point to someone who can help him.

4. Ask the helper to put the pillow under the "sick" child's head and to cover him with a blanket. Then set the bowl and washcloth near the sick child's head. Ask him to close his eyes and then have the helper gently sponge his forehead and cheeks with the washcloth dipped in warm water.

5. Ask for another volunteer to be the pretend sick person and continue with other rounds of gentle caretaking.

Want to do more?

You can set up a make-believe "hospital" in the dress-up area where two or three children pretend to be ill.

Involving parents

Parents can ask children to place a damp washcloth on their forehead when they have a headache or need to relax.

Hospital Gifts

Activities like "Hospital Gifts" empower children to be kind to others. Young children have little understanding of suffering in other people. At this age, the emphasis should be on relating their personal experience to that of others. Can they remember when they were sick? What happened? Well, here is someone who is sick. Let's be kind to him.

What to do

1. Contact the pediatric or geriatric ward of a local hospital to see if they would like drawings from children in your class.

2. Ask the children to describe what being "sick" means. Direct the discussion to hospitals and hospital experiences. How do hospitalized sick people feel? Discuss how it feels to be separated from family and home.

3. Tell the children that they have the chance to be kind to some sick children (or elders). Go to the art area and distribute paper and crayons. Ask the children to draw a special picture for someone who is in the hospital.

4. Emphasize the positive feelings that children or the elderly may have when they receive the pictures. Place the pictures in an envelope and mail it to your contact at the hospital.

Want to do more?

Instead of mailing the drawings, you can drop them off when you visit the institution on a field trip. • You can substitute a nursing home for the hospital and give the pictures to the residents. Elders can draw their own pictures to give to the children. • Read *Shoes from Grandpa* by Mem Fox, illustrated by Patricia Mullins (Orchard, 1990).

Involving parents

Parents and children can cooperate on a family drawing to send to an elderly family member who is not feeling well.

People words to use

sick/ill
hospitals
sadness
loneliness
fear
kindness

Center

Circle time
Art area

Things you will need

- Paper
- Crayons
- Large envelope

Food for the Hungry

People words to use

hunger
nutrition
generosity

Center

Circle time

Things you will need

- Paper
- Several cans of vegetables, soup or fruit to serve as extras

Young children who have never known prolonged hunger cannot comprehend the experience of those who have. Young children can, however, understand that they are doing something to help others by bringing the food to school.

What to do

1. Contact your local food bank to make arrangements for bringing in food donations.

2. Write a brief letter to the parents of your children describing your food drive. Tell them the date you would like to have the children bring one can of food to the school for a local food bank.

3. During circle time, discuss briefly the problem that some children and their families in your community have with hunger. Tell them you will send a letter home to their parents asking them to donate a can of food for their children to give to the hungry.

4. Discuss why good nutritious food is important and suggest different types of food that are needed.

5. On the day of the food drive, give a can of food to the children who did not bring one from home. When all the children have arrived, ask them to bring their cans of food to circle time. Go around the circle, each child identifying the food she brought. Thank each child individually. Briefly describe how a hungry person would react to the food they brought. You might say something like, "Oh, those peaches will taste so good. Peaches will help make a hungry person healthy."

6. Try to arrange for your class to bring the food to the food bank. If this is not possible, perhaps someone from the food bank would visit your class to pick up the food and talk with the children.

Want to do more?

Instead of food, the children can bring in an old toy for distribution to needy children during the winter holidays. • Read *Winter Harvest* by Jane Chelsea Aragon, illustrated by Leslie Baker (Little, Brown, 1989).

Involving parents

Parents can involve their children in deciding which food to provide. What food would be the best to choose? A can of peaches is better and more nutritious than a bag of marshmallows.

4⁺

Rescue Chain

Identifying circumstances that are threatening or dangerous is an early step in the development of courage in children. Even though very young children are not capable of real rescues, role playing this aspect of kindness establishes its value.

What to do

1. As an introduction to the activity, tell the children the following story:

   Once upon a time, Penelope Pig decided to go skating on the frozen pond near Butterberry Hill. All of her friends told her, "Don't go skating. The ice is thin, and you might fall in." But Penelope ignored them and went skating anyway. When she was skating in the middle of the pond, the ice broke, and Penelope fell right into the icy cold water. She was trapped in the ice and sinking fast. When her friends saw her, they wanted to go out on the ice to pull her out. But if they did that, then they would fall in, too. They decided to make a rescue chain. Each person held onto the next person's hand as they stretched out to take hold and pull Penelope out. *The End.*

People words to use

rescue
danger
courage

Center

Circle time
Outside

Things you will need

- Chalk or rope (optional)

2. Ask the children whether they would like to pretend to be like Penelope's friends and rescue her from the icy water. Ask for a volunteer to be Penelope Pig. The rest of the children will make the chain.

3. In a large outdoor space, identify a boundary between the shore and the water. You can draw a line with chalk or stretch out a rope. Place Penelope, sitting on the ground, a sufficient distance from the shore to require a slight stretch in the chain to reach her.

4. Tell the rescuers they have only a few minutes to save Penelope. One rescuer is the anchor, who must remain on shore. You may ask this person to hold onto the branch of a tree or the bar of a jungle gym. The rest of the children make a line, hand in hand, to stretch out to take Penelope's hand. If the line breaks, everyone in the part of the line not connected to the shore will have to sit down to be rescued, too.

5. Ask the children to begin. Cheer them on as they form a line and begin stretching toward Penelope. After a few rounds of the game, talk with the children about the dangers present at a lake or pond at different times of the year.

Want to do more?

To add challenge, decrease the amount of time allowed for the rescue and increase the distance between the shore and Penelope. Of course, do not place Penelope beyond the extreme range of the rescue chain. • Another version is to designate two children as the ends of the chain, one the anchor, one the grabber. Play by the same rules as above but blindfold the grabber to simulate a night rescue.

Involving parents

While the family watches television, parents can talk with their children about characters who "rescue" others. They can use words like "brave" or "courageous" in their conversations.

Kindness Coupons

4⁺

In our materialistic society, children typically associate gifts with store purchases. But a gift can also be a service—like helping someone clean up—or a creation—like a drawing or painting. This activity provides a balance to the commercial messages children see in the media.

What to do

1. Introduce the activity during circle time by asking the children to identify things other members of their family would like to receive as gifts. What is a gift? Emphasize that something kind that you do for someone is also a gift. Ask children for examples of what they could do that would be "kind" to other family members. Offer examples from your own experience.

2. Tell the children you will set up a Kindness Coupon store in the art area. (You may have to explain what a coupon is.) They will come to the store to make coupons which they can use as gifts for family members.

3. At an art area table, ask each child to name what he can do that would be kind to other family members. Help the child identify simple activities like "a gentle hug," or "singing a song" or "helping clean up the kitchen." Try to identify a couple of kind acts for each family member.

4. Write each idea on a separate 5" x 8" card. Ask the children to decorate the cards with crayons or magic markers. They might draw a picture of themselves offering the kindness.

5. Put each card into an envelope with the family member's name on the outside. Explain the activity to parents when they arrive and ask them to keep the envelopes for an upcoming holiday or birthday.

Want to do more?

Read *Oh, Little Jack* by Inga Moore (Candlewick Press, 1992).

Involving parents

Parents can give their children their own set of kindness coupons. For example, one might say, "If you give me this coupon before dinner, I will take you out for an ice cream sundae." Parents should only make promises in the Kindness Coupons that they can keep. The children can only cash one coupon a day.

People words to use

generous
giving
help
kindness

Center

Circle time
Art area

Things you will need

- 5" x 8" cards
- Pen
- Crayons or markers
- Envelopes

Blind Kind

People words to use

blind
senses
sight
touch
smell
hear
give
pretend

Center

Circle time

Things you will need

- Blindfold for each child
- Small lunch bag for each child
- An interesting classroom object placed in each bag such as a small stuffed animal, a block, a puzzle piece

This introduction to using a blindfold reduces some of the apprehension children may feel by keeping them seated and allowing them to stay in control. Success with this activity is necessary before introducing other activities that involve blindfolds. The teacher models gentle helping.

What to do

1. Ask the children to close their eyes for a few moments. Talk with them about what it means to be blind. How would they feel?

2. Show the blindfolds to the children. Show them how to put one on. While wearing a blindfold, describe what your other senses are telling you. What do you hear? What can you touch around you? What can you smell? Take the blindfold off and give one to each child.

3. Tell the children that you would like them to pretend they cannot see. You would like to be kind and give them something to touch, smell or hear. Place a closed bag directly in front of each child. Invite the children to put on their blindfolds. Emphasize that they should remain seated.

4. When everyone is ready, tell them to open their bags to find what you wanted to show them. Encourage them to smell, feel and listen to the sounds the object makes. The emphasis here is to experience rather than identify the object.

5. After a minute, tell them they can remove their blindfolds to see what was in the bag.

6. Do not pressure any child to wear the blindfold. Some may need to watch others before they feel safe doing so. If they prefer, children can simply close their eyes.

Want to do more?

If children are ready for a longer experience, ask them to pass their object to the child on their right. After about 30 seconds of exploration, they can pass again. Give directions before they put on the blindfolds. • Read *Nora's Duck* by Satomi Ichikawa (Philomel, 1991).

Involving parents

Parents can introduce "Blind Kind" at home, taking turns wearing the blindfold with their children.

Wishing Well

4⁺

The wishes you offer in this activity can be pure fantasy, or they may reflect your knowledge of what a child really wants to have or do. Regardless, make your wishes for all the children in your group equally important.

What to do

1. Ask the children if they know what a "wish" means. Talk about a few wishes you might have for yourself. Identify someone you care about in your family and tell the children what you would wish for them. Can the children think of wishes they could make for themselves or others?

2. Ask the children to repeat the following poem with you:

   If my mind was a wishing well,
   I'd find a wish that I could tell—
   A thought from me to you,
   A wish for smiles and fun—
   Something you can do
   To warm you like the sun.

3. After one full verse, describe a wish you would like to make for one of the children in your group. For example, you might say, "Sarah, my wish for you is that every morning ten beautiful teddy bears wake you up with gentle hugs and songs of sunshine."

4. Then have the group chant the lines of the poem with you. Ask a volunteer to offer a wish to someone else. Repeat the cycle and continue as long as the children are interested. Be sure to stop before the children become tired. Give the children who did not have a turn the opportunity to offer wishes at another time.

Want to do more?

How about wishes for the entire group? For example, you can say, "I wish our whole group was in the mountains, singing songs around a beautiful waterfall." • Read *The Mother's Day Mice* by Eve Bunting, illustrated by Jan Brett (Clarion, 1986).

Involving parents

Parents can describe their wishes for their children as well as other family members. Send home copies of the poem for parents to repeat with their children. Parents can be imaginative in their wishes. They might suggest shoes that make their children fly or a magic sack of toys that would never become empty.

People words to use

wish
giving
generous

Center

Circle time

Things you will need

- None

Give a Lift

People words to use

gentle
kind
trust

Center

Circle time

Things you will need

- Nothing

Children whose arms are lifted experience gently supportive contact from their peers. Those who do the lifting have the opportunity to offer gentle caretaking to another person.

What to do

1. Talk briefly with the children about the meaning of gentleness. Invite the children to participate in a simple activity which allows them to be kind and gentle to other children in the class.

2. Ask a volunteer to come to the center of the circle and lie down, letting all her muscles relax, just like a rag doll. Gently lift each of her arms and legs, one at a time. Talk about being gentle as you do so. Ask the child not to help you by lifting her arms or legs. You will do the lifting.

3. Invite other children to carry out the same gentle action with the child's arms and legs. After several children have taken turns lifting, ask for another volunteer to pretend to be a rag doll.

Want to do more?

Play the rag doll yourself and invite children—perhaps two at a time—to lift your arms. Praise children for lifting gently and slowly.

Involving parents

Parents can lie on the floor or the bed while their children gently lift their arms.

Flower Power

Be alert to the give-and-take of this activity. Who gives but does not receive? Who refuses to participate? Do not pressure children to give any of their flowers. Generosity should be sincere. Give children a choice.

What to do

1. Invite the children to make special flowers at the art area table. Pass out the materials and demonstrate how the various pieces can be pasted onto construction paper to make a flower. Ask the children to make flowers on two sheets of paper. They can use crayons to illustrate additional details. Make flowers on two sheets of construction paper yourself.

2. When the flower-making activity is completed, and the glue has dried, ask the children to bring their flowers to circle time. Discuss with them the feelings that people have when someone is kind and gives them something. Tell them that you would like to give your flowers to two children in the class.

3. After giving the flowers to two children, ask, "Would anyone like to give one or both of her flowers to another person in our group?" The children then take turns giving the flowers they made to others, if they choose to. Ask the children to thank those who give them flowers.

Want to do more?

Look for opportunities to encourage generosity in everyday relationships in your classroom. • Read *The Worst Person's Christmas* by James Stevenson (Greenwillow, 1991).

Involving parents

Send home several sheets of construction paper of different colors and encourage parents to make flowers to give to their children.

People words to use

kind
give
generosity
special

Center

Art area
Circle time

Things you will need

- Precut paper flower stems, leaves, buds
- Small bottles of paste
- Crayons
- Construction paper

Birds in the Trees

People words to use

protect
shelter
cooperation
safe
shelter
home

Center

Movement area

Things you will need

• Music

There are no losers in this variation of musical chairs. Instead of children sitting on the sidelines, everyone remains involved. Emphasis is on cooperation rather than competition.

What to do

1. Talk with the children about protection. Steer the conversation toward the idea of shelter as a form of protection. Where do birds and other creatures find protection when there is a thunderstorm? How do our homes protect and keep us safe?

2. Tell the children that you have a protection game for them to play. Some of them will pretend to be trees, and others will be birds flying through the forest. When the music plays, the weather is nice, and the birds can fly. When the music stops, the thunderstorm begins, and the birds will have to find shelter under the outstretched branches of the trees. As time goes by, however, there will be fewer trees and more birds. The birds will have to huddle the best they can under the remaining branches.

3. Ask for one-fourth of the group to volunteer to pretend to be birds. The remaining children are trees. Arrange the trees to make a forest, leaving sufficient room for the birds to fly through safely. Tell the trees that they must remain in place. When the music stops, they should stretch out their arms to provide branches for the birds. The birds seek shelter under the branches of any tree.

4. Begin playing the music. Encourage the birds to fly around the forest. When the music stops, tell them to find shelter under or near the branches of a tree. Emphasize the idea of finding protection under the trees.

5. After each round, ask one tree to become a bird. Continue for several rounds until there is only one tree left. If the birds cannot touch a branch, they can huddle close to each other. End by making all the children birds and yourself the last tree.

Want to do more?

Play two different musical instruments to signal nice weather and a thunderstorm. • Read *Kitman and Willy at Sea* by Chris L. Demarest (Simon and Schuster, 1991).

Involving parents

Parents can take their children for a walk in the neighborhood or a nearby park to look for the "homes" that shelter and protect various types of wildlife.

Generous for Us

4+

This activity can be difficult for children accustomed to taking for themselves. Make sure they understand the rule that the only way they can get a cookie is if someone gives one to them. This is an excellent activity at all times. It is especially effective when children are getting to know each other.

What to do

1. Set the bowl in the center of the circle or in your lap, and ask the children if they know what "giving" and "generous" mean. Briefly discuss how you felt when someone gave something to you. Comment that since the children in the class are learning to become friends, you would like to give them the opportunity to give something to each other.

2. Take something out of the bowl and say, "I would like to be kind and generous to Pablo." After giving the gift, ask children if they would like to be kind and generous to someone. A volunteer then goes to the center of the circle, selects a gift— like a cookie—and chooses a recipient. Repeat with other volunteers until all the children have received something.

3. You may have to take a second turn to give a "gift" to someone who is overlooked by the others. Do this with great tact to avoid embarrassing the child. Remind children that giving something to someone is a way of showing affection, showing that you like them. **No one should leave the group without having received at least one share.**

Want to do more?

Use words or actions as a form of kindness. For example, you can hug a child or say something kind.
• Read *The Baker's Dozen* by Heather Forest, illustrated by Susan Gaber (Harcourt Brace Jovanovich, 1988).

Involving parents

Encourage parents to provide opportunities for their children to be generous.

People words to use

giving
generosity
affection
kind

Center

Circle time

Things you will need

- Bowl of handouts or foods

Wonder Wands

People words to use

beauty
gentleness
appreciation

Center

Circle time
Art area

Things you will need

- A dowel rod approximately 14" long for each child
- Decorative art materials (stars, glitter, ribbon, felt tip pens, etc.)
- Glue

This activity encourages children to notice and appreciate what they think is beautiful around them.

What to do

1. Ask the children to describe what they think "beauty" means. Can they identify something they think is beautiful? Point out that people find different things to be beautiful. Provide a few examples of people who have different opinions about what is beautiful.

2. Show them a dowel rod. Tell them that they are going to decorate the rod to make pretend magic Wonder Wands. Describe the materials set out in the art area. "We can pretend that these Wonder Wands are like magic. We can gently touch something we think is beautiful with the wand and perhaps part of that beauty will become part of the Wonder Wand."

3. At the art area, work beside the children to make your own Wonder Wand.

4. When the wands are completed and the glue firmly dried, call the children together to show off their creations. Teach them the following poem to recite as they gently touch something they think is beautiful.

   Here is a lovely thing;
   Of its wonder I will sing.
   My Wonder Wand will help me find
   A place for beauty in my mind.

5. Touch something with the wand and repeat the chant. Then ask a child to do likewise. After several children have a turn, encourage the entire group to explore the surrounding area with their Wonder Wands.

6. At the end of the school day, tell the children that they can take their Wonder Wands home. They can bring them back to school another day if they wish. Before dismissing the children, describe several things that you touched with your Wonder Wand and why you want to remember these things. Encourage children to identify what they touched.

Want to do more?

Consider touching each child in your class with the wand while reciting the poem. • Read *Good Times on Grandfather Mountain* by Jacqueline B. Martin, illustrated by Susan Gaber (Orchard, 1992).

Involving parents

Children can take their Wonder Wands home to show their parents. They also can teach their parents the poem and show them how to make wands.

No Stranger to Danger

4+

Courage depends on evaluating danger and choosing an effective response. Understanding why an object or situation may be dangerous is an important basis for intelligent action.

What to do

1. Talk to the children about the idea of keeping oneself and others safe. Ask the children for their ideas about what is safe and what is dangerous. Make sure they understand that "dangerous" means that something **might** hurt you if you are not careful.

2. When you think the children understand these concepts, show them a pair of pictures, one showing something "safe," the other something "dangerous." Ask, "Which of these two things is more safe than the other?" When one child responds, ask him to tell the group what makes one thing more safe or dangerous than another.

Want to do more?

Read *Smudge, The Little Lost Lamb* by James Herriot, illustrated by Ruth Brown (St. Martins Press, 1991).

Involving parents

Parents and children can go on a search throughout the house to find objects that are possibly dangerous, such as a knife, electric outlet, matches.

People words to use

safe
danger
courage
brave

Center

Circle time

Things you will need

- Five pictures from magazines of things likely to be dangerous, e.g., knife, fire, gun, electrical outlet, fan, broken glass
- Five pictures of things likely to be safe, e.g., bug, kitten, baseball mitt, teddy bear, chair

Staying Safe

People words to use

safety
danger
rescue
careful
protect

Center

Circle time

Things you will need

- Five or more pictures of potentially dangerous places, e.g., busy street, beach, bathroom, kitchen, automobile, stairs, or cliff.

Differentiating between reasonable and unreasonable danger is an important part of courage. No matter how unreasonable we think they may be, children's fears are part of their experience of the world. Without belittling their fears, we should encourage them to evaluate whether a fear is reasonable.

What to do

1. Ask the children to tell you what they think "safe" and "dangerous" and "careful" mean. Can they give examples of these terms? Tell them you are going to show pictures of places that **could** be dangerous if a person were not careful.

2. Show them one picture and ask, "What could be dangerous about this place? What do we have to do to be careful?" After the children give some ideas, summarize and add key points that you want them to consider.

3. Go back to each picture and create a circumstance in which children see a younger brother or sister acting recklessly in that place. For example, "You get up in the morning to make yourself some cereal. You see your little brother climbing up the kitchen sink to open the cupboard. He pulls out some of your mother's medicine and tries to remove the cap. What do you do?" Encourage the children to identify as many responses to the situation as possible. Introduce the term "rescue" to describe their attempt to keep the young person from being hurt.

Want to do more?

Instead of using pictures, verbally recreate a wide variety of situations.

Involving parents

Parents can take their children for a walk in and around the house and neighborhood to find places that could be dangerous. They can discuss how children can keep themselves safe at each location.

Ship in the Night

4+

This activity places greater demands on children by asking them to move with a blindfold on. Movement within the circle ensures safety and provides security for the blindfolded child.

What to do

1. Tell the children you have a blindfold game for them to play. Begin with this story:

   Once upon a time, not far from Butterberry Hill, there was a boat that became lost at night. There was no moon overhead, and it was as dark as could be. None of the sailors on the boat could see. There was a storm coming, and they had to find a safe place to land. Amy knew the people on the boat were lost. So she walked out to the beach and shouted the ship's name over and over again. The kind North Wind carried her voice out to the boat, and the sailors steered toward the sound to safety. *The End*.

2. The children will have the opportunity to pretend to be the boat and the rescuer.

3. Everyone joins hands to make a circle. Ask for a volunteer to be the ship. The ship goes to the center of the circle and chooses a child in the circle to be "Amy" (the rescuer). Blindfold the ship. Ask the circle of children to rotate around the ship while singing, "Here we go, around and around —find your partner by her sound."

4. Both the rotation and the chant stop at the same time. Standing in the circle, "Amy" begins saying the ship's name, over and over again, while the ship tries to approach and make contact with her. Other children in the circle remain quiet as they protect the ship from leaving the circle. Any child who is touched can gently direct the ship in the correct direction.

Want to do more?

To simplify the activity, be the North Wind who gently steers the ship toward Amy. The ship's task is also easier if the circle is smaller.
• To increase the difficulty, the other children in the circle can make rainstorm noises to complicate Amy's rescue.
• Read *The Bells of Santa Lucia* by Gus Cazzola, illustrated by Pierre Morgan (Philomel, 1991).

People words to use

blind
safety
rescue
protect

Center

Circle time

Things you will need

• One blindfold

Involving parents

Parents can blindfold their child and then, from several feet away in the same room, begin quietly call- ing him. Parents and children can take turns switching roles.

Helping, consideration of others

Know Talk

People words to use

help
talk
communicate
sign language
describe
motion

Center

Circle time

Things you will need

• None

Be prepared to experience some frustration when trying to communicate without words with children. As with other sensory deprivation activities, working through their frustration is an important part of the experience.

What to do

1. Ask the children to tell you why being able to talk is important. How would they feel if they could never talk with words? Mention that some people cannot talk because the parts of their bodies that make a voice do not work correctly.

2. Introduce the idea of sign language: talking with hands and other parts of the body. Demonstrate several examples and ask the children to identify what you are trying to tell them:

   Shake head yes
   Shake head no
   Shake a tight fist and make an angry face
   Wave goodbye
   (Extend both arms as an invitation to hug.)

3. Tell the children that you want to find out what it would be like to be a person who cannot talk in their classroom. When you finish describing this activity, you will pretend for the rest of the morning that you cannot talk. If you have something to tell them, you will say it with your hands and facial expression.

4. For the rest of the morning, if speaking is necessary, motion to another teacher or aide to talk for you. At the end of your experiment, discuss with the children what happened.

Want to do more?

Invite the children to explore how they make sounds. Ask them to touch their throats while making different sounds, talk while pinching their noses shut, or talk with their tongues sticking out. Emphasize that many different parts of the body contribute to making speech sounds. • Invite a sign language expert to visit your class and teach the children a few basics of that language.

Involving parents

Parents can play a similar game of sign language with their children. With older children, they can try signing an entire conversation over dinner.

Seeing I's

4+

This activity adds more uncertainty to the experience of wearing a blindfold. Wearers will have to be patient while their helpers provide them with objects to explore. Children will have the opportunity to both receive and give assistance.

What to do

1. Tell the children you have another kindness activity involving a blindfold for them to try. One child will wear the blindfold while his partner finds things for them to feel, hear and smell.

2. Ask each child to find a partner. Give the pair a blindfold and a paper bag. Ask them who will be the helper and who will wear the blindfold.

3. Ask the helpers to find four interesting objects for their blindfolded partners to feel, hear and smell. Ask them to put the objects into the bag and keep what they select a secret.

4. When they return, help them put the blindfold on their partners. When the children are ready, the helpers can open the bag and give one object to the child to explore. After about 30 seconds, tell them they can hand over the next thing they found.

5. To reduce distraction, discourage the children from talking too much during the activity.

6. When all the objects have been shared, the children can reverse roles.

Want to do more?

Show the children how to hand something gently to someone who cannot see. Blindfolded children can be startled by a partner who drops objects into their hands.
•Emphasize the idea that sometimes people do not want help. Blind people, for example, learn to explore the world and find things on their own. Avoid creating the impression that handicapped people are completely dependent on others. • To simplify the activity, prepare bags ahead of time with three or four items for children to hand to their partners.

Involving parents

Parents can repeat the activity with their children at home, taking turns being the helper.

People words to use

help
blind
senses
sight
touch
smell
hear
give
pretend

Center

Circle time

Things you will need

- One small paper sack and one blindfold for every pair of children

The Goonfalla Trap

People words to use

rescue
courage

Center

Circle time
Movement area

Things you will need

- Small rug
- Stuffed animal or doll
- Blanket
- Rope
- Several large wooden building blocks

Children act courageously when they face a real or imagined threat and do their best to respond to the problem, whether it involves resisting a bully or touching a strange looking bug. These moments of courage contribute to a child's sense of personal power and self-esteem. Be alert to these moments of personal courage demonstrated by children.

What to do

1. Begin the activity with the following story:

   Once upon a time in Butterberry Hill, Amy felt very sad. Her little dog Sparkles was missing. Sparkles didn't come home for dinner. Amy looked everywhere in Butterberry Hill but could not find him. She looked on and around Moonsweep Mountain. Sparkles was not there. Then...ugh! She went to the edge of Stinky Swamp. There in the middle of the swamp on a little island that stuck up from the slurpy, dirty water was Sparkles. He looked so sad. He couldn't leave, though, because his little island was surrounded by the Grumpy Goonfallas. They were hungry, too. They were asleep, but Sparkles was too afraid to leave. As long as he stayed on the little island, the Grumpy Goonfallas could not get him. Well, Amy saw this and knew she would have to get Sparkles before the Goonfallas woke up. So she said some brave words to herself: "When you are afraid and think you might cry, say 'I will do what I can; I will stay and try.'"

   Very carefully, so as not to touch any of the sleeping Grumpy Goonfallas, Amy tiptoed through the slurpy water [dramatize this some]. When she arrived at the island, she picked up Sparkles and tiptoed back to the shore. Then she quickly ran over Moonsweep Mountain right back to Butterberry Hill. Whew! She had rescued Sparkles. Was he ever happy. And hungry too! *The End.*

2. Ask the children if they know what "rescue" means. Take a few moments to discuss their ideas.

3. Set the rug in a corner of the room. The rug is the small island in the middle of Stinky Swamp. Place the rope about ten feet from the island to mark where the swamp water ends. Set the stuffed animal (poor little Sparkles) on the rug. Place blocks (Grumpy Goonfallas) between the shore and the island. The Grumpy Goonfallas are sleeping. With one touch, though, they might wake up!

4. Invite the children to rescue Sparkles by walking around the Grumpy Goonfallas, picking up Sparkles and returning to shore. A child who touches a block must

go to the island and wait to be rescued by another child.

Want to do more?

If you do not have large building blocks, use rolled up towels or folded blankets for the Grumpy Goonfallas. • Increase the difficulty by increasing the number of Grumpy Goonfallas and setting them closer together. • Instead of a stuffed animal, a child can pretend to be Sparkles.

Involving parents

Parents can introduce rescue themes in their dramatic play with their children. They can also talk with them about courageous actions reported in the media.

The Touch Toe Path

People words to use

feet
touch
help
gentle
depend
lead

Center

Movement area

Things you will need

- Various textured materials: a square of plexiglass with no sharp edges, rug samples, sandpaper, a square of plywood with no splinters, a wet towel placed on a plastic garbage bag, a dry towel, small rocks spread out on a large cookie tray, four bricks sandwiched together (watch out for stubbed toes), a piece of furry cloth, a sheet of tin foil, an artificial grass mat, a small folded blanket, leaves spread out on a large cookie tray, a large sheet of paper
- Blindfolds
- Two chairs

By guiding their partners down a path, children help someone dependent on them in a controlled, safe situation. Encourage partners to walk slowly down the path.

What to do

1. Create a multi-textured path and set a chair at both ends of the path.

2. Gather the children in a circle near the path. Tell them that you have created a Touch Toe Path for them to walk down. They must walk with their shoes and socks off, with a blindfold on and with a partner helping them.

3. The children select partners and get in line behind the chair at the beginning of the path. One child from the first pair sits and removes his shoes and socks and is blindfolded. Emphasize to the helpers that they should gently and slowly lead their blindfolded partners down the path. Show them how to put one hand on the partner's back or shoulder while holding the other hand. Ask them to watch their partner's feet and tell him when he needs to step up to avoid stubbing his toes.

4. When the children finish the walk, their partners should help them sit in the chair at the end of the path and remove the blindfold. They can return to the beginning and repeat the activity, switching roles.

Want to do more?

Older children can take partners for barefoot walks in the school play yard during warm weather.

Involving parents

Parents and children can take each other on "Toe Touch Walks" around the house.

Get Well

4+

Refocusing children's attention to someone else's feelings and perceptions is an important step in encouraging them to move from egocentric to sociocentric thinking. Encouragement is based on understanding another person's goals.

What to do

1. When you find out that a child is too ill to come to class, tell the parent about this activity and ask if the child is well enough to receive a telephone call. If not, skip the call and just do the drawings. Arrange for the parent to pick them up or for someone to drop them off at the child's home, perhaps another parent.

2. Gather the children into a circle early in the day and ask them if they know who is missing. Talk about why the child is absent. Take a few moments to let the children talk about the various illnesses they have had.

3. Tell the group that [name the child] is probably unhappy that she could not come to school. Ask the children to think about what they might be able to do to cheer her up. Invite them to visit the art area to draw special pictures to be collected and sent to her. You can write special messages from the children directly on the drawings. Let the children decide what they want to draw.

4. When the drawings are completed, gather the children around a phone. Tell them you would like to call the sick child and let them say some kind words. Ask them what they think would be kind to say. Make the call and let each child who wishes have a minute of conversation.

Want to do more?

Each picture can be a little story that the children make up as they draw it. The teacher can write the story as it is told and attach it to the drawing.

Involving parents

Parents and children can pick someone to call on the telephone who is not feeling well or might benefit from the personal contact. Talk about this person before you call. After the call, emphasize the good feelings it created. Ask parents to think about the type of encouragement they give their children. How do they cheer their children, who are trying hard to succeed?

People words to use

cheer
encourage
kind words
missing
absent
unhappy

Center

Circle time
Art area

Things you will need

- Paper
- Crayons
- Watercolors or felt tip pens

Sheet Carry

People words to use

rescue
gentle
cooperate
protect
help

Center

Circle time
Movement area

Things you will need

- One large, sturdy bed sheet or blanket
- Two small rugs

Avoid being too scary when you set the mood for role playing rescue and protection activities.

What to do

1. Talk for a few moments with the children about the meaning of "danger" and "rescue." Give examples of each. Introduce the activity with the following story:

   Once upon a time in Butterberry Hill, Penelope Pig was watching television when she suddenly smelled smoke. Oh no! There must be a fire in the house. Penelope was so scared. She ran down the steps to get outside, but then she fell and hurt herself. She could not get up to walk out of the house. Casey and Amy saw the smoke and called the fire station. When the fire fighters arrived, they found Penelope and carried her out of the house on a blanket. *The End.*

2. Tell the children you have a similar rescue activity for them to try. One child will pretend to be Penelope who is hurt and unable to leave the burning building; other children will pretend to be fire fighters who make the rescue. Fire fighters will have to carry Penelope to safety on a sheet.

3. Ask for a volunteer to pretend to be Penelope and six to eight children to be rescuers. Take Penelope to one side of the room and ask her to lie down on one of the small rugs and pretend to be injured. Tell the group that this rug is inside her house. Penelope cannot move or help the rescuers in any way.

4. Take the fire fighters to the opposite side of the room and give them the sheet. Lay the second rug down and tell the group that this is the hospital. Their task is to run over to Penelope, stretch the sheet out on the ground next to her and gently lift her up and onto the sheet. Then they should gather around the sheet to pick it up and bring her to the hospital. Demonstrate, if necessary. The remaining children can cheer the rescuers on.

5. Stay with the rescuers to make sure Penelope is carried safely. Be especially careful to protect the child's head when she is lifted onto the sheet.

6. Provide opportunities for all children to participate in the rescue.

Want to do more?

Read *Fabian Youngpig Sails the World* by Ingrid Ostheeren, illustrated by Serena Romanelli (North-South Books, 1992).

Involving parents

Create a similar play situation at home with parents "rescuing" the child from various dangerous situations. Parents can talk about a time in their lives when they did something courageous.

Sad Person

4⁺

Even though children are not giving away something they own, the act of choosing and handing something to another is important practice for generosity. Make sure children are aware of the other person's pleasurable response when receiving a "gift."

What to do

1. Place the items to be distributed in the bowl. Cover the bowl with cloth.

2. Ask the children, "What are some friendly things people can do for you when you feel sad?" Emphasize offerings like hugs, playing a game, taking you somewhere, in addition to material things like buying a gift or making you something good to eat.

3. Tell the children that you are going to give them an opportunity to be generous to somebody pretending to be sad. Set the bowl in front of you and remove the cloth.

4. Ask if anyone would like to pretend to be sad. Ask the volunteer to go to the center of the circle. Ask him to pretend to be sad. How would he act if he were really sad? While the child is pretending, ask the remaining children to chant with you:

Sad Person, Sad Person,
It's okay to feel sad and blue.
Can someone in our group be kind to you?

5. The Sad Person is asked to point to or name someone in the group. This person goes to the bowl, selects a "gift" and brings it to him. The Sad Person then returns to his place in the circle, and the child who selected and gave the gift can pretend to be the Sad Person. If not, the teacher can select another child. The chant and the activity are repeated.

Want to do more?

Be aware of the children who are not selected. Take a turn being the Sad Person and choose a child who is likely to be overlooked. Make sure every child has the opportunity to be the Sad Person. Never tell a child who to pick. Some children may be selected more than once. This is acceptable, but no child should have more than one turn to be the Sad Person. • Read *Mufaro's Beautiful Daughters* by John Steptoe (Lothrop, Lee and Shepherd, 1987).

Involving parents

Children can bring home copies of the Sad Person chant. Parents and children can repeat the activity at home.

People words to use

generous
giving
sad
loss

Center

Circle time

Things you will need

- Bowl of handouts or foods liked by children in your group (cookies, trinkets, sugarless gum, etc.)
- Cloth to cover bowl

The Star Seat

People words to use

cheer
encourage
appreciate

Center

Art area
Circle time

Things you will need

- Sheet of felt to drape over the back of a chair
- Stars of different sizes cut from yellow felt
- Assorted decorations
- White glue
- Small chair

This activity provides a special moment of affirmation for a child. Choosing the right time and child is important. The cheers are for the child because that child **is** special. The cheers are not based on success. They are unconditional. Everyone is a star.

What to do

1. Drape the felt sheet across the art table and set out decorations and glue. Tell the children that you need their help to make a blanket for a Star Seat. Invite them to glue the various stars and decorations onto the felt blanket.

2. When the blanket has been completed and the glue completely dried, bring it to circle time. Drape it over the back of a small chair next to you. Tell the children that this is a Star Seat.

3. Ask for a volunteer to sit in the Star Seat. After the special person sits in the chair, mention some of the things you appreciate about that person. Invite other children to do likewise. Tell the group that you want them to cheer and clap when the person in the Star Seat gives his name. Ask the volunteer his name and start cheering. Raise your hands when you want the cheering to stop.

4. Conduct no more than two Star Seat cheers during a single circle time. Be sure to give every child an opportunity over a period of time.

Want to do more?

If a child makes a negative comment about someone in the Star Seat, respond with something like, "Yes, that upsets you when _____ does that. Right now we are thinking about the things we appreciate about _____."

Involving parents

Parents and children can do home cheers. Anyone can nominate someone else in the family, or family members can ask for cheers for themselves.

Look, No Hands

4⁺

By placing yourself in a dependent position, you empower children to help. Let other teachers or administrators know about this activity in case they stop by to visit. Be sure there is an extra aide or parent in the classroom on this day.

What to do

1. Talk with the children about the special needs of handicapped people. How do we help someone who cannot see or cannot hear or cannot walk or cannot talk?

2. Tell the group you would like to see what it would be like to be a person in the class who cannot use her arms or hands. Tell them that, for the rest of the morning, you are going to wrap an ace bandage around your arms to bring them so close to your body that you cannot move them. Emphasize that you are pretending. You can remove the bandage at any time if you have to. You are okay.

3. Ask the children or another teacher for help in wrapping the ace bandage around your arms so that they are held comfortably to your body.

4. Tell the children that you will need their help because you cannot use your arms or hands. Talk for a few minutes about what you may need them to do. Mention that you have a few ace bandages they can use. Emphasize that although you are going to keep your bandage on for the rest of the morning, they can remove theirs whenever they wish.

5. Call the children together when you remove the bandage. Ask for their help. Take a few moments to talk about what happened and how you felt during the experience.

Want to do more?

Try living with wrapped arms at home for about the length of time that you will have them on at school to make sure you can complete the activity. If it proves too frustrating, give up the use of only one arm and hand. Keep a few extra bandages in case children would like to handicap themselves for a short while.

Involving parents

Parents can try the same activity for a short period of time at home. Children can help with simple tasks like making lunch or tying a parent's shoes.

People words to use

handicap
help
depend

Center

Circle time

Things you will need

- Ace bandages

Know Hear

People words to use

help
deaf
hear
handicap

Center

Circle time

Things you will need

- A comfortable device, such as earmuffs, that completely covers the ears

Although you cannot experience what it really feels like to be deaf, you can role play being a deaf person. Children will have to adjust to accommodate your loss of hearing. This activity may frustrate children anxious to tell you something while you pretend to be deaf. You may have to direct their comments to another teacher.

What to do

1. Ask children why hearing is important. Discuss how deaf people communicate through sign language and lip reading. Ask the children, if they were deaf, how other people could give them the following messages:

   It is time for dinner
   It is time to go to sleep
   I like you
   Goodbye

2. Tell the children you would like to find out what it would be like to be a person who cannot hear in their classroom. Ask them to listen to the sounds around them. Then have them cover their ears with their hands for a moment and listen. How does it feel not to hear well? Tell them you are going to wear ear covers so that you cannot hear well. You are going to pretend to be deaf for the rest of the morning. You will need their help. If they want to talk to you, they will have to use their hands and bodies to tell you what they want.

3. Put on the ear covers and continue with other activities. (Yes, you will look a little silly in July.) When the children talk to you, reply, "I know that you are talking to me because I see your mouth moving. I am pretending not to hear you. You will have to **show** me so I can see what you mean."

4. Call another circle time, take off the ear covers and share your experience with the children.

Want to do more?

Ask someone who can sign to visit your class and demonstrate the skill. Your visitor can teach children a few simple statements in sign language, such as "I love you." • Try dispensing with the ear covering. This situation is more realistic but potentially more confusing for children who find it difficult to remember that you are "deaf." • Read *Amanda's Butterfly* by Nick Butterworth (Delacorte Press, 1991).

Involving parents

Ask children to see whether their parents can guess three messages that they pantomime: "I love you," "I am hungry" and "I am happy." Parents can create their own simple messages to sign to their children.

Gentle Breeze

4+

In this activity, children work together to provide a gentle, comforting experience for a classmate. This may be an excellent opportunity for a child who is overlooked and ignored by others. Do not pressure any child to participate.

What to do

1. Talk with children for a few moments about gentleness. How would a person be gentle to a baby, a flower or a puppy?

2. Begin the activity with the following story:

   Once upon a time in Butterberry Hill, Casey was very tired after a long day of playing with his friends. He stretched out to rest under the most beautiful tree. In just a few moments he was fast asleep. The kind tree felt sorry for Casey. Its branches gently drifted down and lifted him up to rock him back and forth. But when a storm arrived, the tree gently returned him to earth so Casey could run home. *The End.*

3. Ask a child to volunteer to be Casey. She lies down on her back with her arms at her sides and legs together. Ask for eight to nine children to be branches on the tree. These children kneel on both sides of the "tired" child. She closes her eyes. The branches slide their hands, palms up, underneath her back and legs. The teacher should position herself at the child's head, securing her head, neck and upper spine.

4. On the teacher's signal, the branches slowly lift the child from the ground until they are standing. As they lift, the branches make a quiet wind sound.

5. After the child is lifted, the branches slowly rock her back and forth in unison while repeating after the teacher, to the tune of "Rockabye Baby":

   Rockabye person, in the treetops,
   When the wind blows the branches will rock,
   When the storm comes the branches will fall,
   And down comes the person, branches and all.

6. On the last line of the chant, slowly lower the child until she is resting on the ground. Ask the branches to remove their hands slowly.

7. Repeat with another volunteer as the "tired" child.

Want to do more?

Children in my groups were quiet and serious whenever they lifted one of their classmates. If they start acting silly, remind them how important it is to be gentle and careful.
• The "tired" child can choose the "branches" to do the lifting.

Involving parents

A mother and father working together can lift a child into the "Gentle Breeze." During a family reunion, a group of adults can work with children to lift and rock another adult.

People words to use

gentle
kind
cooperate
comfort
secure

Center

Circle time

Things you will need

• Nothing

I'm Mobile

People words to use

help
disabled
paralyzed
handicap

Center

Circle time
Art area

Things you will need

- One sheet of paper for each child
- Bowl of crayons
- Paste
- Collage materials, in individual cups

This activity conveys to children that they can ask for as well as offer help. Requesting help is part of the social fabric of give-and-take, not a sign of weakness.

What to do

1. Set the art materials on a separate table, well away from where the group meets.

2. At circle time ask the children if they know what "help" means. Discuss various ways that people can help each other. For example, if someone drops a bag of groceries, people nearby can help pick them up. Or, if parents have a big task to do at home, their children can help them complete it. Tell the children you have an activity for them that involves helping each other.

3. Ask the children to identify things they can do with a sheet of paper. For example, they can draw on it, cut it, paste something onto it, fold it into something and so on. Take a sheet of paper and say, "Let's pretend I am someone who cannot walk. I do not have my wheelchair with me and need your help. I would like to draw a picture on this paper. Can someone help by getting the crayons for me?" When a volunteer returns with the crayons, thank him and then draw a simple picture. Ask the volunteer to return the crayons to the art table.

4. Ask the children to choose a partner and decide who will pretend they cannot walk and who will be helpers. Hand out paper to the children who cannot walk. Ask them to think of something they would like to do with the paper. After a few moments, tell them to ask their helpers to get the materials that they need. They should bring only one type of thing at a time. When they are through, the helpers should return the materials to the art table. After a while, the partners should switch roles. Tell the children that they can complete their projects after the group has finished meeting.

5. When both partners have had the opportunity to ask and receive help, summarize the activity by saying, "Sometimes we really like to get help from other people, and sometimes we like to be helpful." Give examples of children who helped. Then say, "Sometimes we don't want help, and sometimes we don't feel like helping. Everyone needs help at some time, though. Helping others who need our help is important."

Want to do more?

Make a chart with children's names and a list of repetitive tasks that need to be performed in the classroom. Assign simple work roles to children on a weekly basis on the chart.

Involving parents

Ask parents to look for opportunities to ask children for help even if they do not really need it, for example, washing dishes or opening a door when the parent's arms are full.

Giving Free

This activity should be conducted only after a snack or meal. Recognize children's spontaneous generosity. Giving is based on feeling comfortable and secure with what is owned. Do not force children to give what they want to keep. Emphasize the pleasure to be gained by doing something kind and respond positively to their efforts.

What to do

1. Tell the children you have a giving activity for them to do. Take out the bag of cookies and say, "Here is a bag of _____ that I am going to give to someone in the group. When this person gets the bag, he may decide to keep them all, give them all away, or give some away and keep some. When he is finished, we will talk about what happened."

2. Give the bag to one of the children, choosing a typically generous child the first time you introduce this activity. When he is finished with the bag, ask the children who received cookies to raise their hands. Talk about how they feel. Ask those who did not receive anything to raise their hands and encourage them to say how they feel.

3. Try to help the children understand that sometimes other people will not want to give things to them. Explain that they may feel

sad since it is not fun to be left out. Also tell them that if they are patient, and if they ask, they may find someone to be generous.

Want to do more?

Give two bags simultaneously to two different children. • Or begin the activity by choosing the shyest or most isolated child in the group to receive the cookies. • Read *Country Bear's Good Neighbor* by Larry Dane Brimner, illustrated by Ruth Tietjen Councell (Orchard Books, 1988).

Involving parents

Parents can encourage generosity by helping their children gather old, unneeded toys and clothes to give to charity. Parents can demonstrate their own generosity by giving personal belongings to others and discussing their reasons with their children.

People words to use

kind
giving
generous
patient

Center

Circle time

Things you will need

- A bag of small, nutritious cookies (about as many as there are children in the group)

Night Train

People words to use

help
protect
cooperation
teamwork

Center

Circle time
Movement area

Things you will need

- Extra belts or ropes cut to serve as belts
- Three hats
- Three blindfolds

"Night Train" combines three different but complementary skills. The engine has to **protect** the cars as it moves through the forest, while the trees provide warnings. The engine and cars have to **cooperate** to remain intact as the whole train moves. The train is delivering the toys to **help** children in the town.

What to do

1. To introduce the activity, read *The Little Engine That Could* by Watty Piper, illustrated by George and Doris Hauman (Platt and Munk, 1954).

2. Tell the children that they are going to pretend to be a train bringing toys for children who live in a town on the other side of a forest. But this train is moving at night, and only the engine has a light to see.

3. Ask for a volunteer to be the engine and three others to be the train cars. The remaining children are trees in the forest. Leave enough room between the trees to ensure safety. Tell the trees that they are not to move. They can make an "oooo" sound if any train car is about to bump into them. Place hats on three of the trees. Tell the engine they must go around the trees with hats before they can leave the forest.

4. The cars line up behind the engine and hold onto the belt of the person in front of them. Provide belts or a loop of rope if necessary. When the train is ready, blindfold each of the cars. Emphasize that the engine should move slowly. Supervise closely.

5. Stand on the other side of the forest and tell the train you are the town they have to reach. Ask them to begin.

6. Let the children take turns being the engine.

Want to do more?

To increase the challenge, operate two trains at the same time (if you have enough children), add more cars to the engine and/or bring the trees more closely together. Increasing the difficulty requires closer supervision. • You may also conduct the activity without blindfolds in a darkened room or outside at night. Give the engine a flashlight.

Involving parents

Parents and children can take turns being the engine for a "family train" that chugs around the house. The train cars can be blindfolded as described above. If a young child is the engine, one adult should not be blindfolded.

Caretaking, gentleness, consideration of others

Sprain Pain

Keep in mind that the focus of this activity is the effort to give and receive help, not accurate medical care.

What to do

1. Ask the children if they have ever had a sprained ankle or elbow. Explain what happens when someone has a sprain.

2. Ask for a volunteer to pretend to have a sprained elbow, wrist, knee or ankle. Provide an explanation for the injury. A sprain of the ankle, for example, might have occurred while running across a field and stepping into a small hole. Demonstrate how to drape the bandage around the joint and secure with the metal tabs.

3. Ask the children to find a partner. One will be the injured person and the other, the caretaker. Ask the partners to decide which of them has the pretend injury and where he was injured: ankle, knee, wrist or elbow. Give the caretakers an ace bandage and ask them to wrap the injured person's joint. Provide assistance where needed.

4. When they are finished, switch roles to give everyone an opportunity to help.

Want to do more?

Simplify the activity by shortening the length of the bandage and assisting helpers with the wrapping.
• Read *The Good Stepmother* by Marguerita Rudolph, illustrated by Darcy May (Simon and Schuster, 1992).

Involving parents

Ask parents to loan you ace bandages to reduce expenses. Parents can role play the injured person at home, and children provide the first aid.

People words to use

care
gentle
sprain
wrist
knee
ankle
elbow
joint
handicap

Center

Circle time

Things you will need

• One ace bandage for every two children

Dream Catcher

People words to use

dreams
nightmares
generosity
sleep

Center

Circle time
Art area

Things you will need

- Yarn, thread or embroidery floss
- A hoop made of plastic, wood or metal

Keep in mind that sharing distinctly differs from giving. Sharing means the temporary loss of a personal belonging that is eventually returned. Giving means giving up the object forever. Avoid confusing the two when talking to children. For example, you give a cookie to someone, but you share your truck. Thanks to Ida Nemic of Ironwood, Michigan, for instructions for "Dream Catcher."

What to do

1. Before conducting this activity, make your own Dream Catcher to show the children.

2. Talk with the children about dreams and nightmares. Describe some of your experiences as a child. Show them the Dream Catcher you made and discuss the Native American custom of using Dream Catchers to prevent nightmares. The spiderweb Dream Catcher is hung near the bed to catch bad dreams as they pass through. Good dreams always find a way through the holes in the web. The traditional Native American Dream Catcher was made with a circle of willow branches tied with grasses or reed. The design was woven with grasses or raffia.

3. Tell the children they can make a Dream Catcher to give to someone they would like to help sleep more comfortably. In the art area, help them through the steps to create their own Dream Catcher:

Step 1. Tie your yarn (or whatever material you have chosen to use) onto the edge of the hoop.

Step 2. Loop the yarn **under** and then over the edge of the hoop at desired intervals. The closer you space the yarn, the finer the web will be. Pull it tightly after each loop until you have circled back to the first loop.

Step 3. Now loop your yarn **under** and **over** the center of each loop as shown in the illustration. Continue threading yarn through the centers until you reach the middle.

Step 4. Pull tight and tie off. You now have a simplified version of the Native American Dream Catcher.

4. When they give their Dream Catchers to another person, children should tell them about the Native American custom of hanging these webs near the bed to catch bad dreams.

Want to do more?

If looping the yarn is too difficult, simply crisscross the yarn around the hoop to form a simple web. Note: With young children use yarn; older children can use thick thread or embroidery floss more successfully.

Involving parents

Parents and children can make Dream Catchers to give to each other.

STEP 1

STEP 3

STEP 2

STEP 4

Yay Say

People words to use

compliments
encourage
group
volunteer
relationship

Center

Circle time

Things you will need

• Nothing

The purpose of this activity is to provide practice in giving compliments. Even though the situation created is artificial, "Yay Say" reinforces a norm of kindness and encourages more spontaneous forms of support.

What to do

1. Begin the activity by saying, "Sometimes we have a hard time telling other people what we like about them. Can you tell me something you like about your mothers? About your fathers? Let's think about what we like about others in our class." Discuss the meaning of the word "compliment." Would anyone like to hear what others like about them?

2. When a child volunteers, say, "Chris would like to hear what we like about him. I will start. 'Chris, I like your bright smile when you come to class in the morning. That smile really cheers me up.'" The statement you make should be clear, specific and honest: "I like the way you try to help other children when they can't do something; if I need help I know I can count on you," is better than "You are nice to other people."

3. After you finish, invite other children to describe what they like about the person receiving compliments. If someone voices a complaint, you can respond, "Yes, that is something you want to tell Chris, but this is a time for talking about what we like about others. Dan, what does Chris do that you like?" If a child cannot think of anything, introduce a few of your observations about this child's relationship with the volunteer. "Dan, you really seem to enjoy Chris's company when you ride bikes together. Do you like to be with Chris when you play on the bikes? Is that true?"

4. To avoid wordiness, focus on only one volunteer each time you initiate this activity.

Want to do more?

Begin by asking the children to tell what they like about you. • Or, after several comments, ask the child being complimented to identify something he likes about himself. As children become more comfortable complimenting others, this activity can shift entirely to identifying personal strengths. • Children who cannot think of complimentary things to say to others are good candidates for receiving compliments.

Involving parents

Parents can involve children in spontaneous "strength bombardment." One family member begins by giving a compliment or expressing appreciation to another. Others follow with their own supportive comments to the family member who spoke first.

Taste Helpers

5+

Although this activity is described to children as a guessing game, the primary emphasis is the gentle and helpful behavior children offer while feeding their partners. It also provides a safe situation for children to wear a blindfold. Check for food allergies before engaging in any food activity.

What to do

1. During circle time, tell the children you have a guessing game for them to play with a partner in the snack area. One partner wears a blindfold, and the other selects one of three foods to feed the blindfolded partner.

2. Set out bowls, spoons and cups of water. Invite the children to find a partner.

3. Partners should sit close together, facing each other. After sitting, the child who will taste the food should be gently blindfolded. Partners take a spoon and decide what to give the blindfolded child. Emphasize the gentle behavior needed for feeding.

4. After carefully tasting what their partner selected, the children guess what it is.

5. After tasting the three types of food, the partners switch roles.

6. Ask the children to take their time. They should taste the food carefully before guessing and drink water between samples. They should use a clean spoon each time.

Want to do more?

Make the activity more challenging by increasing the number of foods. Add variety by changing the types of foods. For example, offer five or six different types of raw vegetables or fruits. • Read *Vegetable Soup* by Jeanne Modesitt, illustrated by Robin Spowart (Macmillan, 1988).

Involving parents

Parents can repeat the activity at home. For example, one parent can select food for a child to feed the other blindfolded parent.

People words to use

helping
gentle
partners
trust

Center

Circle time
Snack area

Things you will need

- Bowls of applesauce, pudding and fruit cocktail
- Bag of wooden or plastic spoons (about four per child)
- Paper cup with water for each child
- Blindfold

Touch Me

People words to use

gentle
touch
trust
blindfold
behavior
partner
switch

Center

Circle time
Science area

Things you will need

- Collect an assortment of objects with textured surfaces: furry cloth, sandpaper, crumpled piece of paper, smooth stone, rubber ball, silk.

Children are challenged to touch another person's face in a way that their partners will experience as gentle and sensitive. Children who choose to be blindfolded show trust in their partner's kindness.

What to do

1. During circle time, show the children the tray of objects. See whether they can identify each one. Tell them you have a guessing game for them to play in the science area. One partner puts on a blindfold. The other partner gently touches the blindfolded child's face with an object. The blindfolded partner then guesses what is touching her skin.

2. Place the tray of objects on a table. Invite the children to find a partner. Supervise closely.

3. Partners should sit close together, facing each other. Once seated, the child to be touched is gently blindfolded. Partners choose an object and then gently touch it to their partner's cheek. Emphasize gentleness. Demonstrate touching and supervise to ensure safe and gentle behavior.

4. After thoughtfully considering the object's texture, the children guess its identity.

5. After three or four objects, partners switch roles.

6. Encourage the children to take their time to feel the object rather than rush to guess its identity.

Want to do more?

Increase the challenge by adding more objects. • Decrease the challenge by having children place the objects in their partner's hands.
• Read *Dads Are Such Fun* by Jakki Wood, illustrated by Rog Bonner (Simon and Schuster, 1992).

Involving parents

Parents can repeat the activity at home, taking turns with their children to be blindfolded.

Cats and Mice

Children may have to be reminded to be gentle during this activity. If you find yourself continually correcting them, simplify the activity. Some children are uncomfortable with intensive physical contact.

What to do

1. Cut strips of red and yellow construction paper. Tape the strips together to make child-size headbands. Cut circles from the yellow paper and triangles from the red. Attach two circles to the yellow bands to make enough mouse ears for half the children. Add the triangles to the red bands to make enough cat ears for all the children, minus one.

2. Introduce the game of "Cats and Mice" to the children. In this game, cats do not eat mice—they hug them. To begin, the children are divided equally into cats and mice. Give the cats a red headband and the mice a yellow headband. When the music begins to play, the mice and cats walk around the room, squeaking or meowing. When the music stops, the cats must find a mouse to hug gently. Cats may hug each other, but must have at least one mouse in their "hug bunch."

3. After the cats and mice hug briefly, choose one mouse to become a cat. Take this child's mouse headband and replace it with a cat headband. Start the music and continue as before.

4. Continue adding cats to the group until you only have one mouse left. When the music stops, everyone will be in one big group hug around one mouse.

Want to do more?

Play as a cat yourself and seek out mice that need a hug.

Involving parents

Parents can play a game of "huddle hug" with their children. At any time, one family member will announce, "I need a huddle hug." Everyone immediately runs to that family member to crowd together to give him a hug.

People words to use

hug
gentle
group

Center

Circle time
Movement area

Things you will need

- Red and yellow construction paper
- Tape
- Scissors
- Music

Roly-Poly and the Kind Fairies

People words to use

protection
rescue
danger
escape
guide
safety
boundary
helper

Center

Circle time
Movement area

Things you will need

- Blindfolds
- Timer
- Two 20′ lengths of rope or twine
- Large blanket or sheet

Young children have problems guiding others safely because of their egocentrism. They use their own point of view to avoid obstacles, but are less likely to see through the eyes of those they guide. They may pass safely under the branch of a tree without realizing that it will smack the taller, blindfolded person they are guiding. This activity challenges children to consider the point of view of others.

What to do

1. With the two lengths of rope or twine, mark off the boundaries of a path about three feet wide and at least twenty feet long. This is the bridge. Place a large blanket or sheet at one end of the bridge to be the "island."

2. Introduce the activity at circle time with the following story:

Once upon a time near Butterberry Hill, there was a terrible fire on an island in Moonmist Lake. All the animals on the island were in great danger. They tried to run away but there was no place to go. A long and narrow rock bridge provided the only escape off the island. But the animals were afraid. There was much smoke, and the night was dark. They could not see at all to cross the bridge. The water was too deep to swim. Roly-Poly the Bear prayed for someone to help him and his friends. As the flames grew closer and closer, he felt someone kind and gentle take him by the arm. "I am your friend, your protector," he heard a Kind Fairy say. Even though they could not see where they were going, Roly-Poly and his friends were led safely across the bridge by the Kind Fairies. *The End.*

3. Tell the children you have a game in which they can try to give the protection and help that Roly-Poly received. Point to the path and tell them that it is the bridge. At one end is the island and at the other end, safety.

4. Half of the children volunteer to be animals, the other half, Kind Fairies. Tell them that, because the animals cannot see in the dark and smoke, they will be blindfolded and led across the bridge to safety by the Kind Fairies. Once the blindfolds are on, start the timer. The object of the game is to lead all the animals across the bridge before the timer goes off. Helpers should be careful not to let the animals walk over the boundaries of the bridge. Demonstrate how to lead a blindfolded person gently.

5. After helping the animals put on their blindfolds, ask them what kind of animal they would like to be. Give each child a helper to guide him across the bridge.

6. Once the animals have been led to safety, they may remove their blindfolds and switch roles with their rescuers. When everyone has had a turn, talk about the rescue.

Want to do more?

For an additional challenge, add sharp curves to the path, increase its length or make it narrower. • Shorten the amount of time to make the rescue. • Read *The Boy Who Held Back the Sea* retold by Lenny Hort, illustrated by Thomas Locker (Dial, 1987).

Involving parents

Parents can play a similar game with their children. For the island, use a bed, and for the bridge, large sheets folded and stretched end-to-end on the floor. Parents and children can take turns being Roly-Poly and the Kind Fairies.

No Walk

People words to use

help
handicap
pretend
crutches
wheelchair

Center

Circle time

Things you will need

- Ace bandage
- Crutches or wheelchair (optional)

Make sure that adult assistance is available. Activities that temporarily disable your senses or ability to move have three complementary goals: to challenge children to adjust their expectations in order to help, to provide the teacher with a personal experience of physical disability, and to strengthen relationships between teacher and children.

What to do

1. Contact a local medical supplier, describe the activity you hope to do with your class and ask whether they would lend what you need for the day.

2. Talk with the children about the special needs of handicapped people. How do we help someone who cannot see or hear or walk or talk?

3. Tell the group you want to see what it would be like to be a person in the class who cannot walk. Tell them that for the rest of the class day, you will wear an ace bandage wrapped around your legs so that you cannot move your legs or feet. Emphasize that you will pretend to not be able to walk. You could remove the bandage at any time if necessary. You are okay.

4. Wrap the ace bandage around your ankles to hold them comfortably together.

5. Tell the children that you will need their help because you cannot walk. Talk for a few minutes about what you may need them to do. Mention that you have other ace bandages that they could use to wrap their ankles,

too. Emphasize that although you are going to wear your bandage the rest of the morning, they can wear theirs for as long as they want.

6. Getting around is going to be a problem. You may use crutches or a wheelchair or crawl as best you can. If you expect to go outside, you will need the crutches or wheelchair. Arrange with another adult to carry the wheelchair outside, if necessary.

7. Provide supervision for children wearing ace bandages, especially if they need to go up or down stairs.

8. Call the children together. Take a few moments to talk about what happened and how you felt during the experience. Point out ways that they helped you.

Want to do more?

Combine handicaps to increase the challenge. How would children respond to someone who cannot see or walk, or cannot hear or talk?
- Read *The Dragon's Robe* by Deborah Nourse Lattimore (Harper and Row, 1990).

Involving parents

Parents can take their children for a walk around the house and point out the problems that a person confined to a wheelchair might have living there. They can explore the surrounding community to identify the physical barriers and other problems a person in a wheelchair would face.

Night Flying

For this activity, the children must understand such movement commands as move left, move right, move forward, turn around and stop. Be sure the room is entirely free of clutter. Allow children to remove the blindfolds at any time. If there is another adult in the classroom, demonstrate the activity before the children begin.

What to do

1. Begin the activity with the following story:

   Once upon a time near Butterberry Hill, a small airplane was trying to land at the airport. But the night was dark, and the lights on the runway were not working. Amy's dad was in the control tower. He could see the plane on his radar, so he got on the radio and told the pilot what direction to fly in order to land on the runway. The people on the plane were very happy when they arrived safely. *The End.*

2. Tell the children you have a game for them to play about flying at night. One person will be like Amy's dad, guiding another person who is blindfolded and pretends to be the airplane. The helper guides the airplane from one side of the room to a small blanket on the other side. The helper guides only by **telling** the airplane where to go.

3. The children must be sufficiently mature to understand how to move to the right and to the left. Ask the children to stand and gather in a group behind you. Lead them through the directions with their eyes open. Move to the

People words to use

cooperation
guide
rescue
blindfold
right
left
directions
partner

Center

Circle time
Movement area

Things you will need

- Blindfold
- Small blanket

left, stop, move to the right, stop, turn around. Say the directions out loud as you move. Invite one child to stand in front of the group and give them directions.

4. Spread a small blanket on one side of the room. This is the airport. Take out a blindfold and ask if anyone would like to try the activity with a partner. The partners will have to decide between them who will be the guide and who will be the airplane.

5. Put the blindfold on the airplane. When ready, the guide can begin directing the airplane to the airport. He can accompany the airplane but should not physically direct the partner. The teacher should remain close by to ensure safety.

6. Upon arriving at the blanket, the guide may tell the airplane to sit down and remove the blindfold.

7. Repeat the activity, switching roles.

Want to do more?

Children who have difficulty giving verbal directions can stand behind their partners and gently guide them toward the goal, telling them when they arrive. • Children who are proficient in this activity can try "Drop in the Bucket." • To increase difficulty, try having more than one airplane or setting a timer (for a few minutes) to indicate when the airplane runs out of fuel. • To decrease difficulty, try the activity without blindfolds. Whisper to the guide an object or location for the airplane to fly to. The guide then directs the airplane without specifically mentioning the goal. • Read *The Crab Prince* retold and illustrated by Christopher Manson (Henry Holt, 1991).

Involving parents

Parents can repeat the activity at home.

Parachute Rescue

5+

Watch out for collisions if the children are throwing more than one parachute at a time.

What to do

1. Attach four strings of identical length to each corner of the fabric and connect the free ends to the weight.

2. Roll the parachute into a ball, keeping the weight free. Practice throwing the parachute until it opens properly.

3. Gather the children into a circle near a large grassy area outside. Show the parachute and tell them you have a rescue game for them to play. Take a few moments to explore their ideas about "rescuing." Tell them that a jet's engine broke down, and the pilot had to eject before the plane crashed. Unfortunately (gesture toward the grass), the plane was over the ocean. The object of the game is to rescue the parachuting pilot before he hits the water.

4. The children work in pairs to make the rescue. Emphasize cooperation. Each pair has a parachute and a bucket. One child throws the parachute while the other tries to catch (rescue) it with the bucket. Show the children how to throw and catch the parachute. If the parachute lands in the water, the rescuer should run to it as fast as possible.

5. Children should be encouraged to take turns being a rescuer.

Want to do more?

Since the emphasis is on rescuing, you can do all the throwing yourself. • More than one parachute can be thrown to a rescuer. • Read *The Enchanted Wood* by Ruth Sanderson (Little, Brown, 1991).

Involving parents

Parents can play "Parachute Rescue" outside with their children.

People words to use

rescue
cooperation
pairs
teamwork

Center

Outside

Things you will need

- Lightweight fabric cut into 12" squares (like handkerchiefs)
- String
- Scissors
- Small, safe and fairly light objects to serve as weights (a plastic spool works well)
- Small plastic buckets or similar containers

Mama Hen

People words to use

help
protect
rescue

Center

Circle time
Movement area or outside

Things you will need

- Approximately three sheets of scrap paper per child
- Paper sack or box

If children seem confused by activities that include several distinct roles and goals, look for ways to make it more understandable. Use visual cues to help children remember who is doing what. Mama Hen, for example, can wear a fancy flower hat and Mr. Fox, a wool cap. Put whiskers on the fox with makeup or cut a headband with pointed ears out of construction paper.

What to do

1. Make "eggs" by crumpling the sheets of paper into balls.

2. Gather the children into a circle and tell them the story about poor Mama Hen.

   Once upon a time in Butterberry Hill, someone snuck into the hen house and took all Mama Hen's eggs and hid them in the farm-yard. She wants to get them back. But only her Baby Chicks can retrieve her eggs and return them to the nest. Mr. Fox will try to stop them. Can Mama Hen protect her Baby Chicks while they help her rescue her eggs? *The End.*

3. One child volunteers to be Mama Hen and one to be Mr. Fox. The rest of the children are Baby Chicks. The object of the game is for the chicks to bring their mama's eggs back to her nest without being tagged by a fox. Any fox who tags a chick says, "Shazaam!" That chick then becomes a fox. Chicks cannot be tagged if they are hugging (not just touching) Mama Hen. Only Baby Chicks can bring the eggs back to the nest, but they can only pick up an egg when they are not hugging Mama Hen.

4. Set Mama Hen's nest (the paper sack or box) in the middle of the play area. Disperse her eggs throughout the play area. Ask Mama Hen and her chicks to gather around the nest. Tell Mr. Fox to go to the outer edge of the play area.

5. Announce, "Okay, Baby Chicks get Mama's eggs!" At that moment, Mr. Fox can try to tag Baby Chicks not hugging Mama Hen. The game ends when all the eggs have been returned to the nest, or more likely, all the chicks have been turned into foxes.

6. After the group plays a couple of times, relax for a few moments. Talk with the children about helping and protecting.

Want to do more?

The first few times you play, you can be Mr. Fox to help the children learn the rules. • With older children, trying adding a Papa Rooster and a second Mr. Fox. Play by the same rules, but in this version, Papa Rooster can tag a fox and say "Zap!" When that happens, the fox becomes a chick. Like Mama Hen, Papa Rooster cannot be changed into a fox. • It may help to have Mama Hen and Papa Rooster wear different hats. • Read *The Mud Pony* retold by Caron Lee Cohen, illustrated by Shonto Begay (Scholastic Hardcover, 1988).

Involving parents

Encourage children and parents to play rescue and helping games at home. A chair can become a boat in a lake of alligators. Pretend the boat is sinking, and the children have to rescue the parents.

Forest Tag

5+

A game with several rules is easier when played in a dramatic context.

What to do

1. Gather in a circle and introduce the rescue adventure with the following story:

   Once upon a time, there was a great treasure on the other side of Bluestone Forest. Many tried to find the treasure and bring it back to Butterberry Hill. Unfortunately, the trees of this forest were magic. Anyone who touched their branches would be frozen in place like a statue. *The End.*

2. Ask the children if they would like to get the great treasure. Show them a handful of small felt circles (the treasure). Ask for about five volunteers to try to rescue the treasure from the other side of the forest. The rest of the children are trees. (You need at least a dozen trees.)

3. Evenly distribute the trees throughout the forest. Place them fairly close to each other, but their "branches" should not touch even

when they stretch. Tell the trees that they can bend and twist, but their feet cannot move at all. They must stay in one spot.

4. Put the gold chest (cardboard box) on one side of the forest and the pieces of gold on the other. The rescuers start from a spot near the gold chest. Emphasize that if a tree touches them, they are frozen in place. Any child who reaches the gold can return to a frozen child and unfreeze him with a gentle hug, so long as he avoids the freezing touch of the trees. Once they are unfrozen, children can try again to retrieve the gold. Children who reach the gold may take one piece and try to return it to the gold chest. They can keep trying until all the gold is returned, or all the rescuers are frozen in place.

People words to use

rescue
gentle

Center

Circle time
Movement area or outside

Things you will need

- Small circles of yellow felt
- Cardboard box

Want to do more?

Spread out the trees to make the passage easier. • Clump them together to make it more difficult. • Read *Journey of the Red-Eyed Tree Frog* by Martin and Tanis Jordan (Simon and Schuster, 1992).

Involving parents

Ask parents to think of fairy tales that have a rescue theme, like "The Snow Queen" and "Sleeping Beauty." They can check one of these stories out of the local library to read and discuss with their children.

Protection

Farmer Brown and the Rabbits

People words to use

protection
safety
rules
hug

Center

Circle time
Movement area or outside

Things you will need

- Three large paper bags
- Carrots cut from orange felt
- Simple headbands for the rabbits cut from construction paper
- A hat for Farmer Brown

Every activity has at least one role that is critical to its success. That role is often the most difficult to understand. Farmer Brown is the key role here. When children first try this activity, you can play Farmer Brown, which will also enable you to control the tempo.

What to do

1. At the beginning of circle time, tell the children the story about Farmer Brown and the Rabbits.

   Once upon a time, a farmer by the name of Farmer Brown lived just outside of Butterberry Hill. Farmer Brown's favorite food in the whole world was carrots. He loved sliced and buttered carrots, crunchy carrots with a little salt, carrot pie and carrot juice. So one spring he planted a whole garden of carrots. He watered his garden every day and made sure no weeds grew. Finally, the carrots were ready to harvest. Farmer Brown harvested all the carrots he could eat (show the children the "carrots"). Unfortunately, Briarbutton and his hungry rabbit friends knew all about those carrots, too. So when Farmer Brown was not looking, they grabbed his carrots and hopped away as fast as they could. Poor Farmer Brown. He chased those rabbits, but when Briarbutton and his friends hid behind a tree, he could not find them. *The End.*

2. Tell the children: "Let's play a game. I will be Farmer Brown. Who would like to pretend to be the rabbits?" Choose three children to be Briarbutton and his rabbit friends. The rest of the children will be the trees that protect the rabbits.

3. Take three paper bags and set them on the outer edge of the play area. These are the rabbit holes. Spread the carrots on the ground in the center of the circle. Spread trees throughout the play area. Rabbits put on headbands and take their positions by their holes. Farmer Brown puts on her hat and stands near the carrots.

4. The rabbits have to go to the garden, grab one carrot at a time and then run to put it into their holes. If Farmer Brown tags a rabbit, he gets to take and keep the carrot—if the rabbit had one. The rabbit who was tagged has to return immediately to her hole before reentering the forest to get another carrot. Trees protect the rabbits. Rabbits are safe from Farmer Brown as long as they hug a tree. The trees must stand in one place and not walk around.

5. Once the rules are understood, allow the children to play the role of Farmer Brown.

Want to do more?

Make the activity easer for Farmer Brown by increasing the number of farmers who can catch the rabbits.
• Increase the number of rabbits to make their task easier.

Involving parents

Parents can ask their children about their favorite foods and how they like them prepared.

Left Out

People words to use

kind
giving
generous
patience

Center

Circle time

Things you will need

- One nutritious cookie for every two children

This activity challenges children to manage scarcity. Avoid making a big fuss over children who receive no cookies from others. Some children will take this mild oversight in stride. If you act as though they should be angry or sad, however, they may become upset. Do not force or emotionally pressure children to give their cookies to others.

What to do

1. After children wash their hands, pass out a cookie to every other child sitting in the circle. Take one for yourself. Ask the children not to eat the cookie until you tell them they can. Ask those who have a cookie to raise their hands. Tell these children that they can choose to be kind and generous to those who did not receive cookies.

2. Ask those who did not receive cookies to raise their hands. Then say, "Some children do not have cookies. Would anyone like to give some of her cookie to one of them?" Wait for the children to be generous. Ask for children who still do not have any cookie to raise their hands once more. Repeat your invitation. After this second opportunity, break your cookie into enough pieces to give to those who received nothing from other children.

Want to do more?

To increase the challenge, reduce the number of children receiving a cookie to one-third of your group.
- Read *Oomrazoom* by Diane Wolkstein, illustrated by Dennis McDermott (Morrow, 1991).

Involving parents

Encourage parents to try a similar activity when their child has a visitor, giving one cookie to their child and setting another one aside. Parents can encourage their child to give part of the cookie to the visitor. If the child refuses, they should give the other cookie to the visitor.

Princess (or Prince) Gentle

5+

Activities that involve determining a winner or completing a project have an obvious conclusion. You know when to stop. Many of the activities in this book, however, because they have purposes other than winning, do not have obvious endings. Be sensitive to the group's energy level. Finish games before fatigue or monotony sets in.

What to do

1. At the beginning of circle time, tell the children the story about the Meanies:

   Once upon a time, in a land faraway, there were Mean Trolls. People didn't like them because their touch would freeze you like a statue. People were sad to be frozen because then they couldn't move around. They couldn't eat or laugh or play. Sometimes more than one Mean Troll was running around freezing people. They thought it was funny to freeze people. Fortunately, a Gentle Princess came to town. Every time the Gentle Princess hugged someone who was frozen, he could move again. The Gentle Princess could not be frozen by a Mean Troll's touch. Did the Gentle Princess save the town? Let's find out. *The End.*

2. Ask for two children to volunteer to be Mean Trolls and one child to be the Gentle Princess (or Prince). Give the three children distinctive hats or headbands to remind other children of their roles.

3. The game is played like tag except that when children are tagged by Mean Trolls, they are frozen in place until the Gentle Princess hugs them. This has to be a gentle hug with both arms around the frozen person, not a casual touch. Once frozen children are hugged, they can move again. The Mean Trolls try to freeze everyone in the group.

People words to use

rescue
cooperation
hug
gentle

Center

Circle time
Movement area or outside

Things you will need

- Identical hats or construction paper headbands for the Mean Trolls, a different hat or headband (a crown, perhaps) for the Gentle Princess (or Prince)

4. Demonstrate the hug and emphasize how important it is to be very gentle.

5. Mark off the boundaries of the play area. Ask those pretending to be Mean Trolls to start on one side and the Gentle Princess, on the other. The rest of the children begin in the center. Play ends after a few minutes or when everyone except the Gentle Princess is frozen.

Want to do more?

Change the balance of the game by increasing the play area or adding Meanies or Gentle Princesses.
• With older children, consider increasing the number of Meanies and adding a rule that their freezing powers can be taken away if they are tagged by the Gentle Princesses. They then become normal people who can be frozen by Mean Trolls.
• Read *Monster Slayer* retold by Vee Browne, illustrated by Baje Whitethorne (Northland, 1991).

Involving parents

Encourage parents to talk with their children about times when they were scared and people who helped them handle whatever frightened them. For example, when the author was about fifteen years old, he was chased by an older teenager, a stranger, for about one mile. After he collapsed on his bike in his own backyard, his mother came storming out of the house to confront and frighten off the bully. What a rescue!

After-school Monster 79

Aki and the Fox 153

Amanda's Butterfly 182

Amos and Boris 113

anger 85, 92. *See also* emotion expression, emotion problem solving, emotion recognition association 17, 20, 27, 28, 29, 30, 31, 32, 35, 36, 42, 43, 44, 52, 53, 55, 60, 61, 177

Baby Hugs 61

The Baker's Dozen 167

The Bear Dance 86

The Bear's Water Picnic 116

The Bells of Santa Lucia 171

belonging 17, 20, 28, 31, 32, 33, 34, 37, 39, 40, 41, 47, 48, 49, 50-51, 56, 58

Ben and Porcupine 151

Bentley and Egg 62

Berlioz the Bear 149

Best Friends 37

Bigmama's 57

The Boy Who Held Back the Sea 195

Brother Eagle, Sister Sky 150

Burgoo Stew 122

caretaking 18, 2, 130, 145, 146, 147, 150, 151, 152, 153, 156, 164, 183, 187

Christmas Moon 71

Clap Your Hands 98

community. *See* association, belonging

compassion 13

concerting 16

consideration of others 18, 22, 124, 125, 127, 128, 137, 138, 139, 149, 152, 154, 162, 163, 172, 173, 181, 182, 187, 194, 196-97, 197-98, 204

conversation 17, 20, 38, 45, 46, 54, 137, 138, 177

cooperation 13, 18, 21, 28, 33, 37, 39, 40, 49, 50-51, 76, 86, 97, 98, 99, 100, 101, 102, 103, 104, 105, 106, 107, 108, 109, 110, 111, 112, 113, 114, 115, 116, 117, 118, 119, 120, 121, 122, 123, 124, 125, 126, 127, 128, 129, 130, 133, 134, 135, 136, 137, 138, 139, 140, 147, 155, 159-160, 166, 171, 178, 183, 186, 199

Country Bear's Good Neighbor 185

The Crab Prince 198

curriculum strategies 13

Dads are Such Fun 192

danger 169, 170, 194. *See also* rescue, protection

developmentally appropriate 13, 14, 16

disability 38, 42, 44, 45, 46, 54, 88, 149, 154, 156, 157, 162, 172, 173, 176, 177, 178, 181, 182, 184, 187, 196-197

diversity. *See* multicultural

Do You Know What I'll Do? 152

The Doorbell Rang 131

The Dragon's Robe 196

emotion expression 17-18, 21, 68, 69, 71, 75, 76, 78, 82, 83, 84, 85, 86, 91

emotion problem solving 17, 20-21, 70-71, 72-73, 79, 82, 83, 84, 85, 89, 90, 92-93, 141, 179

emotion recognition 17, 20, 67, 68, 69, 74, 75, 77, 80, 81, 87, 88, 91, 179

The Enchanted Wood 199

environment 38, 39, 103, 130, 145, 146, 147, 150, 151, 166, 168, 176, 192

Fabian Youngpig Sails the World 178

Fall is Here! I Love It! 76

Families Are Funny 47

family 47, 57, 152

Family Farm 110

Farm Morning 115

fear 84, 92, 123, 153, 157. *See also* emotion expression, emotion problem solving, emotion recognition

The First Dog 107

First Flight 73

flexibility, 16

friendship 13, 17, 20, 47, 57, 59, 62, 63, 64, 121

Frog, Duck, and Rabbit 118

Full Moon Soup 132

Garage Song 101

generosity 19, 23, 132, 150, 157, 158, 161, 163, 165, 167, 177, 179, 185, 188, 204

gentleness 18, 22, 32, 42, 107, 115, 133, 145, 146, 148, 150, 152, 155, 164, 168, 176, 178, 183, 187, 191, 192, 193, 194, 201-02, 205-06

George and Martha, One Fine Day 27

The Good Stepmother 187

Good Times on Grandfather Mountain 169

Grandma Gets Grumpy 85

The Great Kapok Tree 124

group activities 12

Hansel and Gretel 55

happiness 74, 79, 82. *See also* emotion expression, emotion problem solving, emotion recognition helping 19, 23, 70, 114, 122, 133, 134, 149, 154, 161, 162, 171, 172, 173, 176, 181, 182, 184, 186, 191, 194, 196-97, 197-98, 200-01

I Don't Care 83

Jackie's Lunch Box 33

Jenny's Bear 30

Journey of the Red-Eyed Tree Frog 202

Julius: The Baby of the World 59

kindness 13

King of the Playground 128

Kitman and Willy at Sea 167

Let's Be Enemies 49

The Little Engine That Could 186

Lot's to Do 100

The Man Who Kept His Heart in a Bucket 74

Mama, Do You Love Me? 90

Monster Slayer 206

The Moose in the Dress 93

A Mother for Choco 147

The Mud Pony 201

Muddigush 102

Mufaro's Beautiful Daughters 179

multicultural 31, 47, 57, 58, 63, 152, 188. *See also* association, consideration of others

My Brother John 84

My Friend John 29

My Mama Says There Aren't Any Zombies, Vampires, Creatures, Demons, Monsters, Fiends, Goblins, or Things 81

names, learning. *See* association

Nathan's Balloon Adventure 154

nature. *See* environment

negotiation 18, 22, 116, 119, 122, 124, 127, 128, 131, 132, 139, 141, 204

Night on Neighborhood Street 76

No Friends 43

No Need For Monty 140

Norah's Duck 162

Oh, Little Jack 161

On Our Way to Market 103

One Frog Too Many 49

Oomrazoom or Go I Know Not Where, Bring Back I Know Not What 204

The Ornery Morning 109

The Owl and the Pussycat 64

ownership 52, 57, 185

parent education 14, 15

parent letters 15, 26, 66, 96, 144

peaceful classroom 12

The Perfect Spot 44

Peter's Song 56

preparing children 13, 16

problem solving. *See* emotion problem solving

protection 166, 186, 200, 201, 202, 203. *See also* danger, rescue

readiness, 16

rescue 19, 23, 159-60, 169, 170, 171, 174-75, 178, 194, 197-98, 199, 200, 201, 202, 205-06. *See also* danger, protection

respect and encouragement 19, 23, 71, 150, 168, 177, 180, 190, 201-02

The River Dragon 127

Rockabye Farm 148

Rosie and Michael 63

sadness 70, 71, 72-73, 74, 79, 83, 92, 153, 157, 179. *See also* emotion expression, emotion problem solving, emotion recognition

safety 12, 16

sequencing, 16

Shoes from Grandpa 157

Silly Fred 82

skills 17-19, 20-23

Smudge, the Little Lost Lamb 169

spontaneous experiences 12

Stars for Sarah 70

Stone Soup 105

storytelling 50, 70, 89, 92, 116, 123, 136, 156, 159, 171, 174, 178, 183, 194, 197, 200, 201, 202, 205

teacher comfort 16

teacher flexibility 16

That Bothered Kate 32

That's Good! That's Bad! 81

The Mother's Day Mice 163

The Quarreling Book 119

The Three Brothers 125

Tiger Watch 141

Time Train 134

Vegetable Soup 191

Voyage Under the Stars 34

Whispering in the Park 28

Will You Please Feed Our Cat 111

William's Doll 68

The Windchild 51

Winter Harvest 158

The Worst Person's Christmas 165